Martial Law

The Memoirs of a kung-F

Volume Two: Toxteth

By the same author

Martial Law
The Memoirs of a Kung-Fu Cop
Volume One: Beginnings

Published in 2001 by New Breed

Photos taken by Steve Richards, Mike Eveleigh, Ken Liu, Bill Wilson. Toxteth images captioned 'Morning after the night before', 'Inferno', and 'Aftermath' taken by Tony Hall 1981, Mercury Press Agency. Layout and photographic scanning by Steve Richards and Bill Wilson. Cover Design: Steve Richards.

Back cover review by Geoff Thompson

Published by New Breed Publishing

Printed and bound in Great Britain.

A CIP catalogue record for this book is available from the British Library

ISBN 0 953855562

Special thanks to Paul Clifton, Editor of 'Combat' martial arts magazine who inspired the author to write this autobiography.

Steve Richards is a biographee in Who's Who in America World, Science and Medicine editions.

Please note: The theoretical information and physical techniques outlined in this book are for Self Protection and Self Defence purposes only. The author and the publishers cannot accept any responsibility for any proceedings or prosecutions brought or instituted against any person or body as a result of the misuse of any theoretical information or physical techniques described in this book or any loss, injury or damage caused thereby.

Printed in Dec 2001 (1st edition)

New Breed Publishing
Po Box 511
Dagenham
Essex RM9 5DN
England

Our Web site www.newbreedbooks.co.uk

Our email address books@newbreed.worldonline.co.uk

Steve Richards can be contacted on: bambootemple@aol.com

Volume Two Contents

Dedication
Foreword
Toxteth
Birkenhead 1982-1984
Final Police Years 1985-1987
Afterlife
Reflections

Dedication

For Pauline

“The Rarest Orchid”

Toxteth

"They Are A Criminal Community… And I Will Police Them Accordingly…"

The summer of 1981 saw the start of Margaret Thatcher's third year in office as Prime Minister. The Tory economic policies where biting deeply into the traditional industrial heartland's of Britain. A curious sense of foreboding was creeping over the country like a dark mist, settling here and there in stifling pockets of tension. The first to give warning of what was to come, were creative artists, writers, and in particular popular musicians. Looking back, it's quite uncanny how the collective psyche was sensed, and given expressive form so accurately in 'pop songs'. Thatcher had given the police a big pay rise of 20% the previous year, which we somewhat cynically accepted as pre-payment for trouble. What none of us realised was how fully we, the men and women of 'Oxford's Blues', were subsequently to be tested on the streets of our own home city.

As fate would have it, just as the first clouds from the coming storm gathered on the near horizon, a magical distraction in the form of the immanent 'fairy tale' wedding of Prince Charles and Lady Diana Spencer lulled the Nations attention away, almost as if in denial. However, these forces were not to be denied…

I was preoccupied with my own forthcoming wedding, only two more sets of Nights to go … and today? Well, just another Saturday on Night duty.

It was Saturday 4th July, the sixth night of seven in the tour and by now my body was getting used to the change in hours –which was fortunate because traditionally Saturday night on the old town was 'busy' and you had to have your wits about you just to get through the shift unscathed. Pulling into the station car park, I noticed how still the summer night seemed – not too chilly, but not warm enough either for 'shirt sleeve order' at least at the back end of the shift, from 04.00 to 07.00. Last night on parade, we'd been read out an enigmatic telex message from Force headquarters saying, 'All police vehicles to stay out of 'E' Division' – which was the South end of the city including Toxteth and the 'Dingle'. Didn't mean much to us, and nothing followed on from it.

The station was busy with 'Bobbie-chat' as it always was at shift changeover time. Nonchalantly I breezed past huddled groups of colleagues deep in anxious discussion – probably about some 'ball ache-r' that had occurred on the afternoon watch. Still, that wasn't my problem, I was here to do my bit, get paid and go home. The locker room was quiet, nobody at all around which was unusual. Maybe the afternoon watch was still out, or my mates where late coming in? As I walked down the corridor to the parade room I heard the rumble of familiar voices, not this time the usual pre-watch banter, but more serious even urgent tones. Walking in I was met with a circle of frowning faces:

'Toxteth's kicked off' said the Cat, grimly.

'What?... What do you mean kicked off?'

'A riot... The Afternoon Section have been called over to Upper-Parliament Street, and we're all on standby to follow'. The Cat spoke like he was delivering a death message, so no 'saucer of milk' ripostes would be appropriate here...

'Shit, Ah well', I said feigning a smile, *'should be fun!'*

My attempt at being jovial worked like a noisy fart at a Women's Institute bring and buy sale:

'Fuck off', said the Maroon Buffoon, clouds of peppermint breath completely failing to disguise the fact that he was pissed.

'I love you too' I said, blowing him a big kiss – thinking that his own favourite trick would irritate him the most in reply.

The rest of the Section where quiet, subdued even…

Deep inside, behind the bravado, I wasn't feeling so light hearted. This was the unknown, and for all its terrors, I'd gotten used to the surprises that 'normal' police duty could bring – without warning. But a riot in Toxteth! That's something that could only be left to the imagination to ponder. The conversation ended, as we started examining the fine details of graffiti on the parade room tabletop, or staring vacantly into the overlapping layers of paper pinned tightly to the notice board. It had never been so silent before we hit the streets. The familiar ritual banter had evaporated, leaving us in a trance.

Our reverie was broken by the hurried entry of the two patrol Sergeants and the Inspector.

Sergeant Mike Warburton was a true blue 'Scouser', he'd never forgotten his roots and had never taken on affectations to further his career. As he sat down to deliver the parade briefing, I could see that his wide staring eyes and gapping mouth where preparing him to give us the news…

A sharp intake of breath and then:

'Ok lad's, some of you will be aware of the situation over in 'E' Division. Following on from last nights telex, there has been a serious outbreak of disorder in Upper Parliament street and the surrounding district. The OSD (Operational Support Division) are fully deployed and need back-up to control the situation. The Afternoon section went over at 19.30 hrs and are still there. It seems that things are being contained, so, we've been told to maintain a 'normal duty' status, but with two men on standby to go over if needed.'

A palpable wave of relief rippled around the room:

'So, the two standby men are... you Cat, and you Steve. Come in for your refreshments at 03.00'.

Feeling that sinking sensation in my stomach, I exchanged grins with the Cat – putting a typical Bobbies brave face on the potential for some very serious personal adversity:

'Well, our families can all sleep safely in their beds now', roared Big Mal, *'Steve and the Cat are going to Toxteth!'*

'No problem', said the Cat, *'we won't be needing you fuckin lot anyway'.*

Inspector Williams rudely interrupted the escalating banter:

'If the call comes through, you will be picked up in the van with the riot shields and handed over to the officer in charge at the scene. You will need to stay there until transport can be arranged to bring you back. Here are the duties for the rest of the watch...'

The Cat and I walked out of the nick together towards our respective foot beats, I was on my usual 'Queensbury Gardens' patch, and he, Grange Road West. Also as usual, we only took nominal notice of where we were supposed to be, and ambled along randomly in the general direction of the Town Centre. I cast a cautious look back over the Mersey towards Toxteth – no sign of burning buildings or smoke maybe everything would be OK? Within 5 minutes of crossing Hamilton Square it was as if nothing had happened – apart that is from making the best of the situation psychologically – after all, we had been selected to be on standby, we were the 'chosen men!' That was status of sorts... wasn't it?'

I had distantly known the Cat since childhood. We had lived within a hundred yards from one another in Prenton. I was the older by about two years, so I had hit adolescence first. My main memories of him were chasing him and his friends around the streets – as older lads do, to establish who was 'hard' (dominant) and who wasn't. I remember being very surprised when he joined the job, as I still thought of him as a little kid, I didn't think he had the guts to be a 'Bobby'. Still, He'd been with the Section for about two years now and he got on very well, and was liked by everyone including me. He had a natural sense of irony, which adapted perfectly to daily Police work. Now though, I was stuck with him as my 'Oppo', maybe to face God knows what in a Liverpool riot. Still, he had proved and was to prove yet again that he had plenty of real-deal 'guts'. A great Lad and a good friend.

Hmm… not quite a saucer of milk, but …!

Three am came, and no call to arms. Walking back into the nick after four continuous hours on our feet came as a relief, we could get something to eat and drink and rest a while….not! Just as my foot touched the step up and into the Enquiry Office I was met by a seriously grim faced sergeant Warburton:

'You're going over, the van will be here from Wallasey in a few minutes, leave your radio's with me, you won't be needing them':

'What about me scoff!' cried a plaintiff Cat.

'Too late, no time for that now it's getting out of hand over there'.

This was real injustice, not even a scoff break! Of course Warburton knew full well that we'd probably bummed our way around all the Chinese takeaways and Indian restaurants, not to mention Night Clubs in the Town Centre, so we were unlikely to starve to death. But, the principle hurt, enough to distract us from our real feelings, and also perhaps our fears…
In the midst of our futile and largely symbolic moans the van rolled up behind us:

'The shields are in the back with the Wallasey lad's', said Warburton.

Taking this kindly as his best attempt at *'goodbye'* and *'take care of yourselves out there'*, we got into the back on the crowded van. There were about twelve of us, two each from the six major parade stations on the Wirral division. The doors were closed and locked. That was that, *'au revoir Birkenhead'*. Looking around there were a few familiar faces but most of them I didn't know. They seemed about as pleased as we were at the prospect of our up and coming adventure:

'What's happening, anybody know' I asked of no one in particular.

'We're being shoved through the pipe (Mersey tunnel) *to stop them getting over to the Wirral'* said an older Bobby.

'Like turds in a blocked drain' added the Cat mournfully.

'*Nice to know that we're so well fuckin thought of !*' I replied.

The journey settled into a resigned silence as we paused at the Tunnel tollbooths. Outside, cars were going to and fro on their normal business as if nothing untoward was happening. Maybe nothing *was* happening; maybe when we got there we'd be sent straight back? Maybe, there really where tooth fairies…

The 'arrival' was a creeping affair, with the van stopping and parking up only to move on in convoy with vehicles arriving from other force areas. At last when we stopped and 'de-bussed' with our riot shields, the situation started to become almost clear. We were grouped like Chess pawns along a wall about 10 yards from a sharp right angled corner. As we watched a 'smoke damaged' Inspector walked around, his face blackened and his uniform covered in no doubt, unwelcome dirt:

'Right, form a line here and when someone falls over take their place'.

'Yer wah!'

'Form a line here so that the officer in front can see around the corner, when someone falls over – replace them'.

'What, is this then, a fuckin Aunt Sally Show!' muttered an old Wallasey Bobby – his face turning blank with incredulity…

'They're your orders, jump to it…', he said turning around and disappearing once more into a bank of drifting smoke.

'Fuckin Hell!', said we all as if with one voice.

Dutifully, of course, we obeyed. The Cat and I where about fourth and fifth in line. Cat obviously thought it was time to make some arrangements for our mutual security:

'Steve, let's stick together on this one, if one of us joins the line the other goes too yeah?'

'Sure, if we're gonna get potted we may as well go down the same pocket'. I didn't play Snooker but I thought the metaphor appropriate.

All too soon we were at the head of the line. I peered round to the right and into Upper Parliament Street. Last time I had been here 'on foot' was nine years previously as a 'skinhead'. How tame those days seemed now! About 50 yards away was a line of Bobbies crouched behind riot

shields, extended right across the full width of the street from building line to building line. On the right and in front of the line where overturned and burning vehicles, to the left; the end block of a formerly grandiose Victorian terrace was on fire. Directly in front and almost lost in a sea of raging rioters, the twisted remnants of wrecked traffic lights blinked pointlessly at random into the night.

Some of the 'Birkenhead Boy's' July 1981

Still trying to take it all in, I became conscious of my riot shield. It was made of a very hard but flexible clear plastic with a high forward facing lip along the top. This was supposed to deflect blows coming at your head, and provide a platform for mounting another shield on top to form a makeshift 'roof'. Ideally, according to the training, we were expected to form 'shield Groups' of four or five officers – three at the front and two at the back. The two at the rear could act as a 'snatch unit' or place their shields on the tops of the other three to make the roof. Well, that was the training, and this? This was the reality… All I could see 'under fire' was the thin blue Line getting the hell beat out of it. Watching the exploding petrol bombs I began to feel uneasy about the foam backing on the shield which was fixed between the grip and the actual shield body itself. If that caught fire it would be 'inconvenient' – to say the least. As for other protection? Our uniforms weren't even fire retardant and for headgear we just had standard police helmets 'strengthened' with a bit of extra cork and internal webbing. 'Oh shit', in other words!

Too late for that now, I shouldn't have had that third vindaloo curry…

I saw a Bobby on the right fall down backwards with such force that he looked like he'd been shot. Quickly, he was snatched away by two Pee-Wee's towards a line of parked police vans doubling as makeshift ambulances.

This was it, in we went!

Cat took up position on my left as we filled the gap in the line, shields forward and interlocking. Through the clear plastic I saw the full fury of the rioters assault coming straight at us. Bricks and paving stones started to beat against my shield. Their impact came as a shock, as in training we had only used light wooden blocks – but this was something else. Inside my mind it became clear that the 'training' was crap and had let us down badly for the 'real event'. The clear shields allowed us to see ahead –but it also caused problems because it goes against all natural instincts to see a brick flying at your face and not to duck or turn away. We had to have a lot of 'faith' in our shields – after all, we'd been told that they could withstand a shotgun blast – but anyway why should we expect one of those in Toxteth?

Cat and I had never felt so close, checking each other constantly as blow after blow rained down on us. It was as if by checking each other we were distracted about ourselves. I felt a very sharp jolt, one that pushed my head so far down that I felt like my neck had disappeared into my body. Cat looked round at me and said:

'You're all right'.

I couldn't figure out whether that was a question or a statement of fact. It hurt like hell anyway. On my right I recognised a

Bobby from the Afternoon section at Birkenhead. In acknowledgement I gave him an appropriately feeble 'deaths head' grin. Suddenly, he dropped his shield in agony and fell off to the right holding his shins. Fleetingly, I wondered superstitiously if I had 'done it to him' through my mock-occult grin. On the ground was a long metal pipe. He'd forgotten to keep his shield base on the floor – and paid the price.

There was no inspired leadership, no initiative, just an obsessional mantra to 'hold the line'. Fatigue eat away at our will and the shields felt heavier with each incoming blow. The worst thing was fire– the petrol bombs. From the comfort of television they don't seem that much, but believe me the prospect of being engulfed in liquid fire is discomforting - to say the least. The man to the left of Cat and the replacement officer to my right were both hit and literally ignited by petrol bombs.

As the hours wore on more and more casualties were pulled out of the line. In the brief respites between sustained attacks, the Lads grumbled openly about the lack of leadership and the natural urge to go forward. But of leadership there was nothing, perhaps it slept. It was getting light by now and on top of an overturned vehicle in front of our line I saw a rioter waving a rice-flail (nunchaku) around with some dexterity. As I looked I thought at first that it was just some kid who was copying Bruce Lee, but then to my great sadness, I recognised him as a member of Master Chan's Hung-Gar Kung-Fu school. Other faces too I recognised hurling bricks and iron railings like spears. At that 'magic moment' I felt a profound alienation. Here I was in

somebody else's fight ,not of my making, and in front of me and against me where some of the people who were supposed to be my 'Kung-Fu Brothers'.

At last some initiative was taken. Not for the last time in the riots, ordinary Bobbies took control when the senior officers demonstrated their impotence and frank incompetence.

The rioters had broken into a nearby dairy and stolen a number of electric powered Milk Floats. Pointing them in the direction of our line. Placing bricks on the accelerator pedal caused them to pick up some considerable speed and hurtle towards us. Their impact could have been fatal.

An OSD Bobby climbed into a police van and pushed through its shattered windscreen with his truncheon. Revving the engine up – and shouting for the line to part he crept forward until a clear path between our men opened. It became obvious to the rioters what was happening. They immediately concentrated their fire on him in a literal fusillade of bricks petrol bombs and iron railings. Bravely he drove straight through and at them. The sight of this bravery roused the lads to move forward with a roar! Futilely, the sergeants and senior officers tried to stop us – but they couldn't.

Faced with this determined charge, the rioters broke and fled. It was over in less than a minute – and obviously could have been hours ago. The Yob's who were cornered fought back, but the hours of pent up aggression determined 'no prisoners!' A quick flurry of blows and it was finished. How much damage and how much injury could have been avoided, if our 'leaders' had shown initiative earlier on? The OSD driver was hailed like a medieval hero. For a while, the senior officers authority was lost in their shame. If we'd have had a flag to raise we would have. Looking around the devastated area, it took on a surreal quality. This was Liverpool?! Some people were going to work and even buses where trying to edge their way through the strewn fields of debris. I saw the shattered remains of some 'unbreakable shields' on the floor, and mused at how we'd been taken in over them also. I was now at the junction of Upper Parliament Street and Mulgrave Street. Turning to my left I suddenly felt a chilling sensation run up and down my spine as I looked up at the burning end terrace Georgian building. Up on the top floor were

'Morning After The Night Before'

The author and the Cat are in the line on the far –left of the following two pictures, after 6 hours of continuous riot duty. Some officers had held the line for more than 12 hours without respite

A petrol bomb ignites a police officer – right foreground of picture…

a family of trapped Chinese! In an instant I was carried back four years to 1977 and the strange dream that I'd had whilst stationed at Upton! Just as in the dream it was daylight, I was in Liverpool in the summer, and there was the burning Georgian house complete with the trapped Chinese family! I felt my facial muscles contort aghast, at the actual realisation of the dreams events. The only missing thing was Mike Eveleigh...and he was going to be my Best Man at the Church in the dream!

'You look like a mad womans' shite' pronounced the Cat, rudely shattering my trance.

I smiled at him thankfully, like he'd given me the highest of compliments.

'At least we got through it' I said benevolently

'Look who it isn't' slurred the Cat.

Following his gaze, I saw the unmistakable green Jaguar car of our beloved leader 'Uncle' Ken Oxford, chauffeur driven as usual by a traffic policeman. Now I understood the slur in the Cats voice. Uncle Ken, it was commonly joked, was permanently pissed. Perhaps that explained his surly arrogance.

For once, the lads did not avert their gaze from him in deference, they looked him straight in the eye, as only men who have proved themselves can against harsh adversity and cold authority. In return he gave his usual disdain. He'd have been more at home as a first world war general that a modern police chief.

'Bang goes his Knighthood' laughed the Cat.

'Yes, Margaret will not be best pleased at this' I laughed in return.

Despite the humour, I was noticing something unpleasant, psychologically. This was a new experience. Was it *really* over? What about tonight? Would we be back again then, would we get through next time? By 10.30am we were preparing to return to Birkenhead. The van was lighter on the return journey. There were fewer of us...

There was no de-brief at the nick, just a casual: *'what happened?'* from the Morning shift sergeant, and a promise that the 'overtime' would be booked in. Driving home, strange feelings of unreality crept over me. I stopped as usual at a newsagent and saw the headlines about the riot. I watched peoples reactions in the shop, there weren't any – it didn't concern *them*. Back home, my father had heard the news on local radio. He asked a few questions but no real emotional support. Maybe it was the 'War' thing again, but part of me felt let down as a 'Son'.

I rang Pauline just to let her know I was safe and then went to bed to sleep it off.

I slept later than usual, getting up at 5.30 pm, just as Pauline called round. No sooner had I got down stairs than the phone rang. It was the station and we were all being called back in for duty immediately. It seemed trouble was brewing again and it was to be stamped out before it developed.

I hardly had a chance to eat and have a shit before I was driving back to work…

In the parade room there was an atmosphere of novelty. Being called in as an 'emergency' tends to bring out a sense of importance and bravado in Bobbies –which was fine but only the Cat and I knew what it had been like, and we didn't feel at all upbeat about the circumstances:

'Give em some stick did yer lad's? asked sergeant Warburton.

'Some. But we took a bit too, in fact it got hairy' I replied.

That was the cue for a bravado born of ignorance:

'Any messin around tonight and they'll get pasted' postured the Maroon Buffoon, puffing himself out to his full circumference. *'Staff the bastards'* yelled Big Mal.

'We'll show 'em, we're not those soft tossers in the Met. We know how to treat Bucks in Merseyside', roared Kid Curry with a voice bigger than his shorter than average height.

The section broke out into a general laugh, leaving only the Cat and I with faint, resigned smiles. I guessed that kind of posturing was necessary to get morale up to the task ahead. And anyway at least we'd ALL be in it together this time.

The whole available section went over – minus the Pee-Wee's who were left with the heavy responsibility of policing the town on a weekend night –normally something unthinkable. They were capable of course, but too few in number, and in the real world no matter how courageous the average policewoman is, she is likely to be physically less tough than the average man. The rising tide of bravado didn't see it that way though:

'Splitarses and squirters shouldn't be doing a man's job', declared Kid Curry.

'Should be at home having kids, that's what they all want really, only join the job to get a husband', said the Maroon Buffoon. *'I should know...'* He said: *'Sadly....!'*

'Sit on my face and make me happy!' laughed the Cat, obviously thinking of a particular Pee-Wee.

The banter was becoming all encompassing, as we prepared to face God knew what next.

On arrival, we were directed to the Force Headquarters in Hope Street. This was easier said than done however due to the enormous amount of police traffic. Double parked right up Leece, Hardman, Myrtle and Hope Street itself, where the largest amount of police vans and personnel carriers that I had ever seen. The streets were jammed with police officer, not just from Merseyside Divisions, but Cheshire, Lancashire, Greater Manchester and yet even more widely located Forces.

Now that was morale boosting!

Surely this meant that Uncle Ken had got his act together and we were going to take full control of the streets.

A Chief Inspector, Glyn McClarnen, who had been my section Inspector at Bebington five years earlier, directed us to go to the main entrance of the headquarters building. We were then sent upstairs to a huge room already packed with scores of Bobbies. With our lot, they

On 'Standby' at Hope St. - The 'Last Line of Defiance'?

must have numbered 120 plus. And then? Nothing....

Time passed and we began to get restless. What was happening? Some Bobbies had transistor radio's, so they were tuned in to the local station: Radio City 194 FM.

What we heard was frightening. The whole of Lodge Lane in Toxteth was on fire. The Nat West bank at the junction with Upper Parliament street had been burned down and a nearby hospital had to be evacuated of over one hundred elderly patients after the building was set alight. The police had lost control with hundreds of rioters running amok. There were heavy police casualties and the Chief Constable had authorised the use of tear gas siege grenades against rioters in the streets for the first time ever on mainland Britain. Further reports claimed that armed police officers were on standby with pump-action riot guns.

We were stunned.

Sergeant Warburton went out regularly to try to get some idea of what we were supposed to be doing, but all he was told was that we were to wait. In that kind of environment rumours start to fly. Some lads from Birkenhead who were on for a twelve hour 3.00pm to 3.00am shift came in for a short break.

'What's the news ?' we asked urgently.

'Pete Streets' missing and Mike Eveleigh is badly injured, he might die. They knocked him down with a shovel and then put his body next to an opened industrial Calor Gas cylinder. Then they threw petrol bombs at it to blow it up.' Pete was a friend...Mike was like my own Brother and of course was due to be my best man at my wedding in September. I was gutted.

The Radio City news continued: *'Rioters are using a mechanical digger to hack at police lines, many streets in Toxteth are alight.....'*

The mood in the room sank, and then arose in anger:
'What the fuck are we here for, we should be out and at em, our mates are getting it out there' cried Big Mal.

'I know Mal, I know' said Warburton quietly, *'but we've got to stay here, they're our orders'*.

This went on and on into the remainder of that night with all kinds of rumours spreading around and all kinds of frustrations being vented.
The news about Mike was confirmed, which devastated me

personally. Then apparently Pete Street was dead, which fortunately wasn't true.

At last Chief Inspector McLarnen (a real Bobbies Bobby) came in. He was sometimes a difficult man to read so we didn't know how to take what he now said: *'What are you lot doing here? We had you down as deployed... You must have been forgotten about'*

That cursory remark raised a torrent of complaints and some frankly abusive statements about leadership and management. McLarnen tried to calm everyone down, and promised to look into things. Time passed...and in he came again:

'You're to stay here', he said. *'Apparently you are the last line of defence for headquarters and the City centre'.*

With that he abruptly left... back into the fray. The lads started to mutter despondently amongst one other:

'Shit, I said, it must be serious...last line of defence...'

'Don't fancy being caught in here if its set alight' said the Cat.

There wasn't much to say in reply, we all knew the implications. The Police Headquarters building had once been a school for the blind. It was a poorly lit rabbit warren - apparently deliberately designed that way to train blind people to find their way around. There wouldn't be much down for us if we got caught in a blaze in there.

And so there we stayed for the duration of that second horrendous night of rioting.

We went back to Birkenhead like a defeated army. The 'Cheshire contingent' of around a hundred men, had virtually all ended up in the Liverpool Royal Hospital as casualties. Our

A battered 'thin blue line' bravely advances through Toxteth's burning streets:

"Inferno"

own lads had taken a hell of a hammering as had the men from the other forces. We felt sorry in particular for the Cheshire lads, being dragged away from villages most of them… only to be knocked down and burnt on the streets of Liverpool.

It was such a shock to us that we now felt we were in a war zone. Maybe it was the beginning of a civil war? After all Left wing extremists and drugs dealers were believed to be behind the rioting. So was this 'payback time' for Tory policies? Was this why Maggie Thatcher had given us that 20% pay rise last year? Were we to be 'sacrificed?'

Going off duty that morning I was like a different person. Survival instincts were taking over from my rationality. I felt hopelessly vulnerable and decided that I'd better tool myself up for the next nights rioting which would surely follow. Before bedding down for some much needed sleep, I sought out an old hunting catapult –made of strong steel, and went up onto a nearby railway line were I knew I could find some iron ore pellets –round and heavy metal ore, just the right kind of ammunition…

Normally under severe stress, sleep was difficult for me, but now it might be a question of survival. I couldn't afford to go back to Toxteth exhausted. So, I slept a long and deep sleep. On getting up, the television was full of the news from Toxteth; film of row after row of burning buildings and pictures of wounded officers. Already the politicians both local and national were making a meal of it.

William Whitelaw as representative for the Thatcher government, arrived at Liverpool Airport. Ken Oxford deliberately drove him through the worst affected areas so that he could see what the Police were up against. Whitelaw was shocked despite having seen service in the Army in World War II. Burning and collapsed building, overturned cars – two square miles of the city were left devastated. He reported back to

Margaret Thatcher that something had to be done…

We were put on permanent twelve-hour 'Night duty' until further notice, so I went in for 18.00 to find many of the lads had got there well before me. A lot of them were tooled up as well: mostly with close range weapons, which I thought useless. If it got so bad that they needed using to save our own or each others lives then I wanted to be able to 'pot' our attackers at an appropriate range. As far as I was concerned someone throwing a petrol bomb intended to kill, and that I wasn't having, not after the last two nights.

We left in the vans as usual, this time we headed outside of the rioting area to St Anne Street Police station 'SAS', as it was known in 'A' Division. In the yard we tried out our various 'tools'. I wasn't the only one with a 'catty', but I had the only really effective ammo. We took pot shots at the warehouse doors opposite the nick. The iron ore was vastly superior in weight of shot and accuracy.

Having been fired up by target practice we were ordered to move out to Lodge lane; the centre of the burning orgy the previous night. The vans stopped at the top of Upper-Parliament Street, and we continued on foot the short distance across the junction with Edge Lane and on into the 'Lodge' itself.

Lodge lane was a ghastly site, like something out of the Blitz. Not only were buildings still smouldering, but some had collapsed across the road or fallen inwards into heaped piles of rubble. Thick swathes of grey-white smoke sharply contrasted with the burnt blackness of the rubble and debris. So thick was the smoke that visibility was down to only a few yards in either direction – including upwards into the buildings. This was hazardous as it provided ambush opportunities. By now we were expecting the very worst. Toxteth was a haunt for armed gangsters and there was now no reason to believe that firearms wouldn't be used against us. Crossbow bolts had been fired the previous night, and OSD 'armoured land Rovers' had been penetrated by 'projectiles' possibly bullets. We kept in 'line of sight' with one another as we had no radio communication. Our only orders were to establish a 'presence on the streets'.

It was eerily silent. So quiet that the slightest noise was exaggerated. As it transpired the only event of the night was a half hearted man – on –man challenge from a local yob, who postured from a roof top, but wouldn't come down to 'play'. Paddy O'Loughlin suggested potting him with the catty, but that wouldn't have been sporting.

So the night ended in relative calm. The area was successfully saturated with Bobbies and maybe, we thought, they had had enough; or perhaps the energy of the rioters had simply been spent. Going home that morning was a 'coming down' experience, off a high of adrenalin and cortisol. I left the 'catty' at home.

The next few nights were much the same. There were a few token attacks, but they were quickly dispersed. There was a massive police presence, and at last, we began to get some decent protective equipment. We were all issued with Green coloured Nato riot helmets, usually deployed in Northern Ireland and basic shin and groin guards. More 'short shields' were issued too. These were the smaller round shields – like something out of medieval Europe, for use by 'snatch squads' who needed the kind of mobility impaired by the full-length variety.

As well as the tear gas grenades and Nato riot helmets we were told that Army armoured personnel carriers 'Pig's as they were known in Ulster, were on standby for our use. 'Uncle Ken' once commented that if Liverpool went up it would be worse than Belfast or Londonderry. Obviously he meant the potential for 'sectarian' violence, but from where we were this could have been the start of something just as bad – maybe even worse. There wasn't any precedent to compare it with, and the escalation suggested by 'Ulster style' equipment just added to our gloom and foreboding. Much of the feeling was stoked up by ex-army lads who'd served in Ireland and who at least pretended to relish the idea of street battles here in Liverpool.

The force also hired fleets of vans from commercial companies to provide transport and deployment capability for our increased numbers. These vans were welcome, but they were rudimentary in terms of trim and equipment and many were not up to the demands of the situation mechanically.

The Salvation Army travelled around the groups of Bobbies with biscuits and tea urns, bringing much needed refreshment. Our mood lifted as we seemed at last to be in permanent control of the streets.

After some days, it was decided to 'stand down' a number of the local, Merseyside men, so that they could take up routine patrol duties on their own patch. Accordingly my section returned to the town. The twelve hour shifts and cancelled rest days however, stayed in force.

Back at Birkenhead Central, we had the air of 'veterans' about us. Not all of our colleagues had been over to Toxteth. None of the policewomen went initially, at least in the front line, although they did sterling service holding the fort on night duty on the town. Some of the men didn't go either, and I felt sorry for them as they only had their imagination to allow them to deal with what might happen if it kicked off again and they had to go over. One 'man' in particular hadn't gone and he'll turn up somewhat ironically, later in our story.

By now the 'copycat' riots springing up all over the country were draining our resources. Moss side in Manchester was in particular; as the Greater Manchester Lads had to be divided up between their own patch and Toxteth. Locally, in Liverpool, Everton, Kirby, and Cantrill Farm had all 'kicked off'. Toxteth itself was still *relatively* quiet. Many suspected that these out of area riots were deliberately orchestrated in order to draw men away from Toxteth itself so the bucks, lefties and drug dealers could regain the initiative.

At Birkenhead Sub-division, our leaders were assessing the possibility of our council estates and urban areas starting too. I was still nominally the 'community beat officer' for the Queensbury Gardens Project'; so, some bright spark had the idea of testing the water there through 'tension indicators'. These weren't really specified, but in my case I was ordered to walk across a square mile of derelict ground towards some tower blocks – with my big hat on – to see if anything happened, if it did, then there was tension! The elegant logic of this was quite lost on me as I approached the flats with all the trepidation of a sacrificial victim!

Not knowing what else to do, I stood upright before the towering edifice that was Queensbury Gardens and waved my arms about. It felt like standing on top of a lightening conductor in a storm – stupid and yet strangely compelling.

Hmmm…maybe that bang on the head on the first night…?

Nothing happened, so in the spirit of the moment I yelled:

'Yoo hoo, Bucks! Here I am!'

Still nothing…

Almost disconsolately I walked back towards the nick. On the perimeter of the derelict ground I met sergeant Warburton and a group of back-up Bobbies. I hadn't been told that they were there, so I feigned courage stifling a laugh at how daft things had become.

As it happened, Queensbury Gardens and its surrounding area was the *only* 'anticipated' place on the Wirral division that didn't kick off – contrary to expectations. I liked to think that my last years efforts at community policing had something to do with that – but then maybe simply no one wanted to play?

Within a few nights we were back on standby in Liverpool again. It had been decided that in order to make best use of our now overstretched resources, groups of mobile 'Police Support Units' (PSU's) would be based at strategically located stations around the force area. Instead of the more usual 12 – 15 man units they were to be doubled or tripled in size, and transport would be provided by the Merseyside Passenger Transport Executive; on single decker buses.

Our unit went to Smithdown Lane, the headquarters for the forces Traffic Division and Driving School, and, the nearest station to Upper-Parliament Street itself. Yet again little happened for a night or two, and then things kicked off on the Wirral, on the 'Ford' estate. This was good news for us, because if things had to happen anywhere then it would be better on our own ground, somewhere we were familiar with. That said, as you will recall from my time at Upton nick, the Ford was not the best place to manage a large-scale disturbance. It was in the Cat's very own words, *'laid out like a mad woman's shite'*. Access to the inner part of the estate was difficult with blocked off roads and concrete pillars. Road names were confusing or missing, and alleyways crisscrossed the area like rat-runs. Lovely!

From reports received one bus load would be enough, and by the time we got there, it had been sorted out by the OSD who found the locals lacked the stomach for a fight with battle hardened Scouse Bobbies. Somewhat disappointed (at least outwardly) we returned to Smithdown Lane Nick.

The following night; Saturday 11th July, we were playing a game of makeshift Cricket with the wickets marked out on a riot shield and a staff (truncheon) used as a bat. It felt like we were a bunch of Battle-of-Britain pilots waiting for the scramble call. Colin Mathews' was batting. He was a curious policeman who'd had a private education and then got himself a Cambridge law degree, just to end up in this job. He was a great lad though, thoroughly reliable, someone who hadn't actually drifted far from his true working class roots. Many of us saw in him a future 'Chief' in the making – and one who would not forget what is was like on the streets.

It was my turn to bowl, just as a message came through to 'scramble' to a very large-scale riot on of all places the 'Woody' (Woodchurch Estate). This was going to be the 'big one' on the Wirral, as rioters had taken control of the estates two largest dual-winged tower blocks and were smashing up residents' flats and stealing their property.

Three bus loads of Bobbies were scrambled, led by motorcycle outriders. Our mood was high as we were looking for a decisive encounter to finish the copycat Wirral riots. So high in fact that the bus driver got caught up in our enthusiasm and nearly turned the vehicle over going around the Junction 3, M53 roundabout alongside the Woodchurch Estate itself. Normally, going around a motorway roundabout in a bus on two wheels would have been hairy, but we were well roused up and hardly noticed!

We approached from the 'blind side' of the tower blocks, only to park in line, and within full view of them. The Upton lads hadn't been able to control the start of the riot, but they did have the support of most of the locals' and we were actually cheered by them as we de-bussed. Within minutes the tea was flowing, as well as other less official beverages. The atmosphere seemed in marked contrast to Toxteth…

The Chief Inspector in charge of the operation was an ex Wirral Traffic Group man: Kevin Fox, a man whose intelligence, appearance and manner suited his name. He quickly sized the situation up: both dual-winged tower blocks were effectively 'occupied' by large organised gangs of rioters – the residents had been forced out and barricades had been erected at the entrances and along the gangways. Attempts by the Upton police to gain entry had been repulsed by a fusillade of missiles and even furniture from as high as the 14th storey. Locals reported 'petrol bomb factories' in both blocks.

So…what now then 'Foxy?'

Chief Inspector Fox, as with most leaders was not always a popular man with his men, but perhaps his hour had come. This was going to call for inspired leadership as well as caution. The sergeants were briefed to deploy their men around the base of the first block: Ferny Brow Gardens.

I was with sergeant's Chris Garvey, our 'station sergeant', and my old 'adversary' and patrol sergeant Pete Townson. Chris Garvey was a 'nice' man, but with a tendency to flap under pressure. He had a lot of service in, and genuinely cared about his men. We walked up the side of Ferny Brow Gardens and came under immediate attack with bricks and broken bottles. Chris's reaction, was to flap, naturally enough. Squatting behind his shield in the middle of the road he chirped frantic orders out, which no one could hear properly – and which were generally ignored. The lads followed Townson up to the top of the road, we thought to do something proactive, but no, he just stopped same as Garvey had done and assumed the 'Aunt Sally' posture behind his shield. Meanwhile, other units had moved to approach the entrance side of the tower block, access was through a gap between two blocks of four storey maisonettes. That was when the ambush started.

The lads approaching the entrance were hit directly by bricks, iron bars and even bags of piss.

Our intelligence sources had neglected to tell us that the rioters had positioned themselves in and around these maisonettes, on the stairwells and balconies. This gave them a good field of fire and the poor street lighting supported their cover.

‘Cometh the hour, cometh the man’, or so it is said.

The hour was now, and the man? PC Bob Smart, my ‘Oppo’ on the Queensbury Gardens Project. Bob of course was an ex - Army officer and had served in street riots in Northern Ireland. I saw Bob and instinctively moved over to him, he gathered a score or more of us around and gave out his instructions:

‘Right lads, what we need here now is discipline and courage. Move straight at ‘em they won’t stand and fight if we don’t stand and let them hit us. Clear the stairways and alcoves – and keep together. We’ll walk slowly until we are about fifteen yards away from them and then we’ll charge!’

We drew our batons and marched towards the gap. I could hear Shakespeare’s’ Henry the Fifth’s speech about ‘once more into the breech..’ spontaneously playing in my mind, but I stopped at the bit where it’s said ‘Or close the wall up with our English dead!’ Hmm…

At Bob’s word we rushed them, which clearly they didn’t expect. He was right, at least insofar as they didn’t want to stand and fight but cornered people will have a go and at last I was at the right range for some martial arts.

As I’ve said before, real street fighting is a curiously ritualised thing, very similar to what you’d get in a troupe of chimpanzee’s; clubbing howling, scratching, biting – running away. In that kind of contact, awareness is as important as hitting potential. It’s easy to get the equivalent of ‘red mist’ and go blind to what’s around you. Get mixed up in any group fight in a relatively open space and you will see what I mean. Some people scan around nervously and hesitate, others plough in with complete disregard.

Economy of energy use is very important. In heavy police uniforms and cumbersome headgear you get worn out quickly. So, hit economically and primarily to make yourself 'safe'. A lot of hits act as blocks in that they stop-hit someone, or encourage them to 'go away' (fuck off in other words). Sometimes, people go rigid and curl up, even in a standing position. Their rigid limbs becoming efficient long-levers for restraint. Restraint can mean an unfortunate collision between their head and a nearby wall, or it can mean them going down to the ground and giving up. You see what I mean of course.

Bob was a natural leader, and as such people do, he took command from those who hadn't a clue despite their 'rank'. I respect Bob, he's a good and honest policeman and a fine man to have around in a riot.

We took no prisoners in clearing the stairwells – which was a mistake. We'd gained ground but the yobs ran off with their injuries and melted into the darkness. They could come again. Still, Ferny Brow Gardens was now surrounded. All we needed to do now was get in!

At this point I was surprised to see the enormous and familiar frame of Georgie 'Gus' Hill. He was the fellow you might remember, who four years earlier had expressed a wish to blow my head off with a sawn-off shotgun. I was glad of my helmet and riot shield:

'Get in there Sir! They're fuckin mad, what about dee's old folks?'

Normally, people simply said 'yes' to Gus, no matter what he was saying:

'What old folk's Gus?'

'They've got em in der – in der flats in Ferny!'

Further sophisticated conversation followed, and it seemed that some pensioners were still in the flats and being 'terrorised'. This was reported to Chief Inspector Fox, who decided that we had to go in immediately. Gus was the biggest 'Yob' of his generation, but even he didn't like what was going on. That meant it had to be bad.

Fox drew up plans to enter the flats using a technique we'd practiced on 'Public Order' training days. It involved units of around 15 officers arranged in a 'Roman Tortoise' formation. This was a boxed in-body of men, with their shields interlocked above and around all four sides. The formation was to approach the doorway, and the lead men were to place their shields up on the lintel (a protuberance at the top) of the door frame. Then one by one the men passed under this makeshift roof and into the building. Great in theory… Now, for the first time *ever* in Europe, a Police Support Unit was going to do it for real, and enter a multi-winged 14 storey block of flats against resistance!

The entrance to Ferny Brow Gardens was barricaded with furniture, which for all we knew was soaked in petrol and ready for ignition. With that less than reassuring thought, we enthusiastically formed the Tortoise – ready to make 'police history'.

As we shuffled along slowly, closer and closer to the entrance, surges of adrenalin anticipated the impact from above that must surely come. With some relief the first hit received was hard but not too heavy, the object rolling off to one side without breaking our formation. Then… all hell hit us, furniture even a gas cooker – ripped out from some poor sod's flat. Some of the ads faltered with the blows, but we naturally felt impelled to pick up speed – like a snail changing gear from first to second…

On reaching the lintel over the entrance we fumbled to get the 'roof up whilst other lads pulled away at the barricade. This was the dangerous moment as we were at our most vulnerable. The Tortoise formation was breaking up to allow officers to breech the barricade, and we were positioned directly beneath the flats with no cover. Any movement by us would be in 'range', and standing still was a no better option. We had to be quick. Rioters were on the first floor landing and foyer and throwing stones and bottles at us. The breech in the first barricade was made and we entered, shields 'proud' to obstruct the rioters fire. Behind, the lads broke up the Tortoise formation in textbook fashion, with the last man holding his shield up on the lintel – all under fire. He must have been hoping that his shield alone wouldn't have to take the full force of a direct hit off the top floor – it didn't, and at last we were all in safely. A brief exchange of close quarter fire and truncheons ensued and the yobs withdrew from the entrance. Having thus secured the foyer, we decided to fan out around the dual wings of the ground floor.

Once again, 'natural leaders arose' – initially no senior officers came in with us. It was decided on the spot to secure each floor balcony by balcony, landing by landing - and then to search each individual flat to 'flush out' the rioters. We knocked on each door in turn, forming a screen of shields, as we didn't know what to expect from inside. If the door opened, we entered immediately and effected a full search. If the door didn't open – it was kicked in. This may seem excessive, but we couldn't afford to allow the possibility of rioters being left behind us as we moved on up the floors. Particularly as the building could have been set on fire at any time, fatally trapping both us and any remaining residents.

Those residents still inside where helped to the foyer, or allowed to stay once we had 'cleared' their floor of suspects. Some yobs did try to hide amongst the honest and decent folk who lived in the flats. Many were identified either directly by the Police or by the frightened residents for whom all hell had broken lose. These yobs were then turfed out – in an appropriate fashion, that is 'advised', in the police colloquial…

At this point other Bobbies began to take their chances and run hell for leather through the gauntlet of rioters missiles into the building. This way, our numbers where gradually built up.

One Bobby broke cover from too far away. As he made his run towards the entrance he looked up at the flats zigzagging as he went. From the top floor an object flopped over the balcony and plummeted downwards. Perhaps this chap had played too much football. His timing was just right. As he looked up he altered course to make perfect contact between his upturned head and the bag of cement. An almost silent explosion of grey-white powder followed leaving a transient but impenetrable cloud. When it cleared the officer was lying prone on the floor- arms and legs outstretched. The whole spectacle left me marvelling at human psychology.

Floor by floor the yobs were forced back. Some who were cornered started to fight by manically beating and kicking at the shields with weapons of various kinds. Once again, within martial arts range it was time for some man-on-man. As before keeping calm and conserving energy was all important. At least this wasn't an 'ambush attack' so to speak, as I was already prepared. Long rioters weapons such as staves had limited use in the tower blocks confined spaces along the narrow balconies. The arc of swing was only practicable from one side, and jabbing or thrusting had to be got right otherwise it

"Steve, what was that you said about the 14th floor ?"

was easy to pass inside. Once you got inside the length of the stave, it became ineffective– the closer you got to the attackers grip the better, and the longer they hung onto it the better too. It seems that many untrained people who attempt to fight with sticks hold onto them way beyond any useful time, perhaps gripping on gives a sense of security, but in reality it ties up the hands so as to make defence against grappling or striking very awkward. Elbow and single knuckle strikes proved efficient discouragers knocking the fight of many a yob.

The main hazards were the open balconies and stairwells. I for one didn't like the prospect of going over the side – it was a long way down! The stairwells left many exposed angles as it's impossible to cover all sides of yourself whilst ascending through a series of open 90 degree turns. There was also the elementary problem of becoming tired by pushing upwards against resistance. Further barricades were met on the landings and along the balconies. Fortunately, no petrol bombs were thrown – although we couldn't have known of that in advance and we had to be continuously alert with adrenalin surges. Gradually, we forced our way to the top, with the rioters in retreat. Finally there was only the 14th floor left. At this point the rioters of Ferny Brow Gardens gave up. But, it wasn't over for them yet…

Officers manned each landing and 'staffed' the yobs down all fourteen flights of stairs until at the bottom they were arrested. By that time they were thoroughly beaten and subdued. We were elated, it had been like storming a castle – and we had conquered!

Chief Inspector Fox was caught up in the relief and the merriment. Suddenly he was popular – and heck… I even saw him smile!

At this point Superintendent Woods arrived. He was obviously pleased at what had happened and affirmed to Fox that his unit had achieved a first for any police force in Europe. However, the job was only half done, there was still Grasswood Gardens, and a hell of a din was breaking out over there.

The residents of the estate where out in force, and all of them at the time, apart from the rioters that is, fully supported the

Police's approach. However, our 'victory' at Ferny Brow did not put off the Grasswood Gardens 'garrison'. On the contrary they seemed full of fight and violence to property. Having done it once, Fox determined to do it again, same approach, with the exception of a preliminary 'Aunt Sally' and 'walk straight into an ambush routine. We felt confident, if tired. The Tortoise re-formed with some fresh men and went in as before – followed by gauntlet running individual Bobbies. Up the stairways, balconies and floors we went – kicking in doors and fighting hand to hand. Once again the defeated were staffed down all 14 flights of stairs and arrested.

There was a slight problem however, in the mutual enthusiasm of the moment, a local councillor and a Methodist minister who out of a sense of religious and political pastoral care; had rushed to the scene, and found themselves being staffed down the stairs of Grasswood Gardens as if they were rioters – how could such a mistake be made? How was it that the police ignored their protestations? How was it that the ****** where there in the first place? These and other mysteries were never to be satisfactorily answered – not even in court…

In the court hearing that followed, most of the rioters were either acquitted or given extremely limited punishment. Little direct evidence was offered by the police, over which individual rioters had been responsible for which actions. The local press made much of the Minister and the Councillor and photographs of some of the lads actually made the front pages.

The lads who stormed the tower blocks felt mighty pleased with their achievements. Having more than proved himself as a 'leader of men', Chief Inspector Fox was liked by everyone for at least a month afterwards, and there was talk of having a commemorative tie made with our units call sign 'Tango Zulu 2' emblazoned across it. Never happened though. Ultimately Bobbies are too individualistic even within their own 'group' culture. Chief Inspector Fox and Superintendent Woods were instructed to submit a full report on the tactics used, which was then to be circulated through Interpol – the international police co-operative and intelligence network.

The long term picture was positive. The local yobs swore 'never again' and there hasn't been anything like it seen on the Woodchurch Estate ever since. Decisive police action had proven to be the key, just what had not happened so far in Toxteth itself.

Meanwhile, on Monday 13th July, Margaret Thatcher herself arrived for a meeting with the local authority in Liverpool City Town Hall. She was shown photographs and film of the rioting and police helmets pierced by staves and railing spikes. Bernard Ingham her private press secretary advised her bluntly that this was an attempt to bring her government down. Then, together with Oxford, she faced Lady Margaret Simey – Chairwoman of the Merseyside Police Authority and 'representatives' of the Toxteth communities.

The meeting was tense to say the least. Thatchers position was stern declaring that:

'The law must be upheld!'

In return, Lady Simey quoted issues of 'race' that she believed to be behind the riots, and also Oxford's famously unhelpful pre-riot judgement of Toxteth:

'They are a criminal community and I will police them accordingly'.

Members of the Toxteth Community present also stood up to Mrs Thatcher citing issues of race as being central, not crime or drugs. Naturally this didn't endear the Prime Minister to them.

The official police position was that it *was* criminal behaviour and drugs dealing that had ignited the lawlessness and rioting.

The meeting ended with Mrs Thatcher apparently determined that the law will prevail, but with some idea about appointing a

‘Minister for Merseyside’. Michael Heseltine was to be handed that particular poison chalice.

We, the ‘front-liners’ watched the news with some trepidation. Our very fate may be being decided politically right at that moment. The impression given by the media was that the rioting had ended. We, of course, new that it hadn’t. Although on a lesser scale, skirmishes were still flaring up in Toxteth every night. Meanwhile across more than 40 other UK Towns and Cities, ‘copycat’ rioting was breaking out.

Whilst all of this was happening, I was temporarily posted as ‘observer;’ on one of Birkenhead’s two fast response cars, call sign: ‘Golf-Romeo Three One (GR31).The driver was Chris Llewelyn, a very experienced Bobby for whom just about everyone had a lot of respect. He had been a ‘Jack’ (detective) but found his way back into the ‘real world’ of front line uniform work on the streets. He was a Class One high-speed pursuit driver – one of the few on the section, and that carried a lot of credibility in the police’s ‘car culture’. It looked like it would be an enjoyable tour of duty…

One GR car always paraded on an hour later than the rest of the shift – in order to provide some street cover during changeover of watches. This meant that the following watch had one GR vehicle that started an hour late. On this particular night Chris and I paraded on an hour after everyone else. We were handed a telex message by Warburton concerning a known drug’s dealers car– a very distinctive Bentley, on a private number plate. This car, and its owner/driver were very involved politically in the riots, and they were frequent visitors to the North end of Birkenhead. The telex said that the driver was believed to be armed and carrying drugs, so if seen, the vehicle should be stopped and searched – with all due caution regarding the likelihood of guns being involved. We’d all seen the Bentley many times before, it was quite blatantly driven around for all to see. Chris decided that we should have a look for it and see if we could ‘lift’ the driver.

Sure enough within two minutes of leaving the nick we turned into Conway Street and coming down the opposite side of the road from the North end of the town was our Bentley!

Chris pulled round behind it and put on the 'blues and two's. The Bentley stopped dead in the middle of the road, and out stepped its clearly irate driver; Leroy Brown. He was dressed immaculately and obviously expensively, in a manner you might expect for a Bentley driver, but not perhaps someone from a working class Toxteth background:

'Mr Brown, I've caused your vehicle to stop because....' Chris was interrupted:

'What the fuck's going on? You've stopped me because I'm a black man, because of the riots, because of what you pigs are doin in Toxteth, fuck off, I'm goin you ain't go no right...

'Because we have information that you are carrying illegal drugs in your vehicle...' continued Chris.

'And, because we believe you are carrying a gun' I said... at the wrong moment... and in the wrong way.

Everything fell silent, I looked deeply into Brown's eyes, he turned muttered and ran the few short steps back to his car...

I'd faced the threat of firearms before, but in that brief moment I saw the ludicrousness of this situation. What had I said? Why did I say it? Why had he started to run to his car?

'Goodnight Mr Brown' said a voice.

'Come on Steve' said the voice again and I felt a hand turn my shoulder round towards the police vehicle.

Looking back Lerory Brown was half in his car giving the single finger 'salute'. Chris and I got in the police car and we drove off:

'Not worth it. Think about it Steve, is he worth it?'

'No', I mumbled, deep in thought – he wasn't.

'Let's keep this to ourselves then. A firearms unit can tackle him some other time'. I've got a Wife and family and you're getting married soon'.

Our morale was at its highest ever and there was a general feeling that the riots had petered out. We couldn't have been more wrong. Towards the end of July, the lull in Toxteth exploded afresh with clearly organised gangs of rioters running amok.

New tactics were to be employed against them. Rather than standing still and taking a battering, we were instructed to deliberately drive police vehicles at the rioters as they assembled in order to break them up. Once broken up, Police Officers on foot would be 'dropped' to arrest offenders and take control of a given area.

This was a new and rather disconcerting development. Men under extraordinary pressure were being encouraged to drive straight at rioters who were hurling bricks, petrol bombs, iron railings and God only knew what else at them. For the most part, these vehicles were plain unmarked hire vans, 'thin skinned' and offering no protection whatsoever to officers. Also, invariably the confrontations were at night and on difficult terrain, perhaps involving the negotiation of burning barricades and road-blocks.

The police vehicles were organised into units of three or four. The first three vehicles would carry uniformed personnel, the last would carry the riot shields and other equipment. Only one vehicle in each such unit had a radio, and the drivers where mostly from outside of Toxteth and didn't know where the hell they were from one minute to the next. It wasn't just badly organised it was crass stupidity. There was bound to be a disaster…

We had been involved in these 'tactics' for about three nights. It wasn't much fun being effectively leaderless and dropped out without radio communication into the middle of a large-scale disturbance. By now enough had happened for a lot of animosity and bitterness on both 'sides'. The police had already suffered several hundred casualties and those of us left felt things had become an issue of survival. We were also aware of the political battle raging between the extreme left and Thatcher's government. How we were all being vilified and 'tarred with many a common brush' by senior members of the Merseyside Police Authority, who seemed to support the rioters, and also the dreadful fatigue that comes when you have to start all over again after believing that it had all finished.

It wasn't just the politicians and the media who joined in the vilification. Ordinary people did too. People who should have known much better. Usually these were middle-class types, professionals who didn't live in an affected area, but maybe they'd had a parking ticket or a speeding fine in the past, and now thought they could revel in the battering the police were getting. This was morale sapping. Superficially because these people represented 'decent' folk, and more deeply because it illustrated fully the truth of the fickleness of human nature.

After such nights on riot duty, I'd go home and see ordinary people, most of whom had never been in a fight or life threatening situation in their whole lives, just carrying on as if nothing was happening. Mentally, I contrasted this to the collective psyche during the last World War. At least then everyone was together against a common foe. But now… *we* were the apparent enemy with few speaking out in support of us. How things would change though if we did lose; how these comfortable people would then have their world turned upside down into chaos and outright anarchy. And you know what? I reckoned that they'd have deserved it…

It was 28th July, the night before the Royal Wedding. Most people were fully preoccupied with that and didn't give a moments thought to the on-going street battles in Toxteth. I had picked Pauline up from work, which would have given me about half an hour to see her before going back on duty. We were driving along Borough Road in Birkenhead when the lights at a pedestrian crossing turned red. I stopped and the car behind us didn't. The impact was severe enough to give me a whiplash injury and to write my car off. Being a Bobby, I sorted out the matter quickly with the other driver at the scene. I was actually anxious to get back on duty, not because it was an enjoyable thing to go to Toxteth, but because I couldn't let my mates down by not turning in. Pauline tried her best to dissuade me – particularly given my neck injury – which hurt like hell and limited the range of movement in my head, neck and shoulders. But I wouldn't have it; grimly, I determined to get in no matter what.

The Birkenhead lads were to parade on at Wallasey that evening, which was the only station with sufficient parking facilities for the numbers of vans required. Whilst waiting to go, my neck injury got even worse, tightening up. Also, there was an element of shock involved; after all I'd been with my Fiancée who could have been seriously hurt, and my car was a write-off. Now, I was about to go hand-to-hand fighting in a Liverpool riot!

In Toxteth, things kicked off as usual after dark. That night it was like a First World War dogfight with vans turning and crisscrossing inside each others paths chasing rioters who hit out with bricks and staves at us. Disembarking, I was in the middle of another hand-to-hand slug-out. I didn't even know where I was, or who was with me. Our Nato helmets made identification of colleagues impossible. The injury was excruciatingly painful and what skills in martial arts I had degraded into feeble defensive jabs with my truncheon.

Having 'cleared' a particular area it was back to the circus like weaving with the vans, which became nauseating. From our vehicle, we saw the curious figure of a disabled youth amongst the rioters. He wore distinctive white trousers and had a pronounced limp. A few nights later he was dead, run down by a Police van.

"Aftermath"

A lone Liverpool Bobby stands guard on the streets of the devastated city

During a respite, we managed to reform into our 'home' units. On this night there were three vans, two personnel and one equipment. The lead van had the radio in it, and we had to rely on hand signals and torches for inter-vehicle communication. Our 'leader' was an Inspector; Tomlinson, who had been a patrol sergeant on my 'streets' section posting as a Cadet back in 1975. He had been an arrogant and aloof man then, and he'd not mellowed with rank or the passage of years. In fact he was incompetent under pressure. What he 'ordered' next was a stupidity that would have won him medals in the Crimean War. We were to drive in 'convoy' up and down Upper-Parliament Street. Why? – a mystery – known perhaps only to his elevated opinion of himself. The effect was that we came under fire from perhaps a hundred rioters from either side of the road. The vehicles took a pounding and windows were smashed in. The Equipment van was at the back with a single Bobby in it – the driver. He had no radio communication and his windscreen had gone in with bricks continually flying through. This wasn't enough for Tomlinson, he decided to do it again, and again. By what turned out to be our final run we were in a state of near mutiny.

Chris Llewelyn was our driver, and he was about to uncharacteristically 'lose it'. A gang of rioters had got between us and the equipment van. They were carrying half a telegraph pole and were charging the equipment vehicle with it. Chris said: *'Right that's it, I've had enough of this shit from Tomlinson'.*

He wheeled the vehicle round, breaking 'formation' and drove straight at the yobs with the telegraph pole. They stood their ground, but Chris didn't flinch. In the back of the van, it was a curious experience to agree with the sentiment but feel dubious about the action. We had absolutely no control over what would happen next.

The rioters dropped the telegraph pole and ran off up a grassed embankment opposite Mulgrave Street, before a maze of maisonette flats. Chris followed, and, the van got stuck…

We were surrounded immediately. The doors ripped open and the windows smashed in. A merciless stream of bricks and lumps of concrete were hurled through. I heard the screams and cries of colleagues as they were hit. Trapped in the crowded van in a seated position I instinctively curled up and forwards to protect myself, at which point I felt a terrific impact on the left side of my head. For a moment it was like an out-of-body experience, with the sense of looking on dispassionately from some vantage point outside and above of the van. I remember a fleeting thought almost as if it were someone else's about this probably being 'it' particularly if the van is set on fire…

I don't remember what happened next. It was as if I was suddenly standing upright outside the van. The rioters had withdrawn about fifty yards . Sergeant Townson who had been in Inspector Tomlinson's van was standing to my left. Around me colleagues were lying on the floor injured. In front and between us and the rioters was a wall of Bobbies behind shields. I saw the van overturned and completely wrecked – a total write off:

'Shit', said Townson, *'you've had a hell of a bang on the head, your helmets stoved in!'*

I put my hand up to the left side of my helmet and felt a huge gapping hole. I went to try to take it off, at which point everything started to get dizzy. I remember being helped to the ground, and then bricks starting to fly over from the direction of the Maisonettes. Next thing I was placed on a shield and dragged sledge-like down the road by a couple of riot helmeted Pee-Wee's acting as auxiliary ambulance staff.

In the Royal Liverpool hospital, the corridors were full of wounded policemen. I felt somewhat guilty because in my case there was no blood, and other officers lying there were covered in it. I was obviously concussed but with enough awareness to realise that I was. Eventually, I was seen by a junior casualty doctor, who ran through the usual tests. I didn't have a knee jerk reflex, but I could follow a moving object with my eyes. When he held up his fingers and asked for a grip test, I found myself acting as if in two minds, I knew what he had asked for and what the task required was, but I gripped his fingers hard and then bent them back and downwards so that he dropped screaming to his knees. I don't know why I did that, it was totally unconscious – maybe a reaction to feeling helpless and trapped in the van – I've never been sure.

I had an x-ray which showed up no fractures and was transferred via Police vehicle over to the Birkenhead General Hospital. Sergeant Townson, turned up later to see how I was. Enmity and dislike suspended for the 'duration' it seemed. He told me Kid Curry was in hospital injured from the same incident as were Chris Llewelyn and five others. He had my riot helmet with him. It was shattered like an egg shell. If I hadn't had been wearing it I'd have been killed. Apparently I was hit by a huge lump of concrete. I was kept in for another day on 'observations' and then signed off injured for two weeks. For me, the riots were over….

In all by the end of the riots some 793 police officers had been hospitalised. Scores more received more minor wounds, the final total of Police injuries topping the 1,000 mark. One rioter had died having been run over by a police van. Others were seriously injured including at least one with a broken back as a direct result of that dubious and dangerous policy of driving directly at people. As many as eleven rioters had been shot with CS gas 'Seige Canisters' designed for penetrating buildings; blowing holes in their bodies – one person had been castrated by such a shot. Two nights before the riots 'officially' began, a police officer in Toxteth had been dragged along the road by a stolen car and smashed into a bus stop. He died. Whilst on sick leave due to injury, one officer died with a stress-induced heart attack.

For years afterwards the stress effects of those terrible weeks took their toll as scores of officers were retired on health grounds due to what would be clearly recognised today as post-traumatic stress disorder.

150 buildings had been destroyed by fire over a devastated two square mile area of the city. 500 rioters had been arrested. More than 1,000 individual crimes were reported.

The total cost in damage to property was at least five times as great as the Brixton Riot's in London. Ten times as many Police casualties were sustained

Margaret Thatcher had stood her ground – only it wasn't literally hers of course…

Thus ended the worst ever riots in mainland Britain and the nearest thing yet to a revolution in modern British history.

Michael Heseltine promised much, but the money went to out-of-area firms. Trees were planted, much to the residents' amusement, and millions went into a'Garden Festival' site – some miles away in Auigburth and Otterspool along a derelict ship breakers site that had been known to me and generations of local kids as 'The Cazzie' – The Cast Iron Shore. Bobbies joked that the only horticultural pursuits indulged in or of interest to the Toxteth residents would be cannabis plant cultivation and 'poppies' for heroin.

Uncle Ken was not best pleased with how he had been criticised for his handling both of the pre-riot situation in Toxteth, and the actual management of the disturbances themselves. He decided to give Toxteth its 'community policing'.

He drew an arbitrary line on the map around Toxteth and effectively made it a Police no-go area, at least for Police vehicles and vans. The area was to be Policed by uniformed foot-patrols – the least pro-active element possible. If a crime occurred outside of this demarcation-soon to be nick-named: 'The Toxteth Triangle' then criminals could only be pursued up to its boundary. Then the chase had to be broken off. Naturally, crime escalated through the proverbial roof. Armed robberies took place at banks just for the robbers to flee into the safety of the 'triangle'. Drug crime soared as dealers and importers sprung up like weeds.

A posting to Toxteth, never the most popular of places to be stationed, now took on an aspect of the insane to it. You'd have to be of doubtful mental stability to 'volunteer' for such work.

The Force Headquarters were moved from Hope Street (200yards or so from Upper-Parliament Street itself) down to new purpose built accommodation at Canning Place by the Mersey. The now abandoned Hope Street became the 'Nick' for the new Toxteth section. Truly, a border outpost in urban bandit country.

Mike Eveleigh was off work for some considerable time following his injuries. The attack on him symbolised for me at least the injustice of collective human rage. You couldn't have got a better or more decent Policeman than Mike. Earlier that year, he'd risked his life by dragging a tree trunk off a railway line – in the path of an oncoming passenger train. The rail line ran past the 'Woody' and it was that Estates yobbish representatives that had placed the obstruction there.

But that was typical of Mike, to risk his life for others – unflinchingly.

Despite his injuries, and the post traumatic shock that hit him and his family, Mike kept his promise to be Best Man at my wedding. If ever the title 'Best Man' was deserved…

Pauline and I were to have a 'mixed' religion marriage – although neither of us could be described as practicing Christians in anything other than nominal form. Canon Burns was officiating for Rome. I lived within the Woodchurch parish, so it was to be Woodchurch Parish Church that was chosen for the Wedding. The church itself occupied a commanding view over the infamous Estate of the same name. It may seem an odd choice to go there, as we could have got married in Pauline's parish at Bebington. However, we'd decided on an Anglican 'venue' with a joint service between the High-Anglican (Anglo-Catholic) and Roman Catholic denominations. Woodchurch Parish Church was an ancient building – Saxon in fact, built on a Celtic Druids sacred grove. As a Church it was beautiful and had a presence and numinosity absent in modern buildings.

The choice of Woodchurch Parish Church, and of Mike as Best Man, fulfilled the last part of that curious and prophetic dream from 1977, that had also seen the trapped Chinese family in the burning building and the massed ranks of police officers in Upper Parliament Street.

The hostility from Pauline's parents continued apace. They even called at Canon Burn's Presbytery to ask him to refuse to bless the marriage and to tell Pauline not to go ahead with it. That was a foolish and vain thing to do. Canon Burns knew me very well, and how I'd worked for his local community. He trusted me, and he also knew Pauline. They were on a hiding to nothing and were given short shrift.

Two day's before the Wedding, Joe said to Pauline:

'Well, what are you doing about this wedding of yours then?'
It seemed that he'd bowed to the inevitable and accepted that what will be will be. Up until that moment we had believed that he wouldn't turn up. John Cain was on standby to 'give Pauline away'. After all he'd been much more of a Father to her in recent years than Joe had ever been.

I'd been hoping for a traditional Chinese Lion Dance outside the church from Master Chan's school, as was my right and as he would have granted. But, there were problems with Ho-Sing's side of things. In the end, I had to accept that it would be better if neither Master were invited. To invite one without the other would have caused endless difficulties – and it was after all Pauline's day primarily. Also, she had some reservations about the reaction of guests at the church - to being met by something as 'pagan' as a Chinese Lion dance troupe just outside the churches lytchgate. I thought it was a wonderful idea!

The day itself went exceptionally well. Pauline looked stunning as ever, Mike was on first class form. Canon Tostevin, the C. of E. priest officiating for the Anglicans looked like something out of a Dennis Wheatly horror novel. Dark, broad and brooding with a literal mop of jet-black hair over his eyes. He had warned us not to film inside the Church as the ceremony was sacred. Tony Carpenter – my old friend, attended as an Usher and film-camera man. Not caring – or perhaps believing in such things, he stood in the Porch of the ancient Church and filmed Canon Tostevin as he approached draped in his black cloak. The Canon flashed him a sideways look of priestly disapproval as he wafted by, at which point the camera inexplicably seized and broke down. The film we have on the wedding is perfect up to that point –just as Tostevin's silvery glance flashes into the lens – then all went dark! Fortunately we had a standby camera and film…

Also present, was the spiritual healer John Cain. Smiling as ever he stood at the back of the Church to watch the marriage before leaving to return to his patients. Many of them made up the congregation – good people – good 'souls' quite literally. Pauline's Mum – Marie, looked like death itself. It was obvious that she was there under duress. She never smiled once just glowered under the brim of her hat. Pauline, fortunately, didn't care. There were plenty of other people around her who were loving and happy for her. It would have been nice of her Mother to have made the day special for her youngest daughter. After all, she had 'prophesied' that Pauline would be a teenage bride, and that is exactly what had happened. Joe though, having accepted defeat, was magnanimous, doing the best he could at the eleventh hour to make things right (at least on the day itself that is). Claire, jealousy abated – again temporarily, acted as Chief Bridesmaid. Old Mrs Baines attended in all of her regal matriarchal glory, and made sure the family behaved itself by waving her walking stick around like a parliamentary mace.

Mike's support extended to taking the official wedding photographs. The day went fabulously well, something good then at last from a hard and bleak year….

Joe Giving Pauline Away

V' For Victory ! '

Wedding Day September 19th 1981

Birkenhead 1982 – 1984

"On the scrap heap"

The new year saw a return to relative normality on Birkenhead's streets after the interlude that was Toxteth. We still had use of the surviving extra hire vehicles, some of which were so badly battered that they couldn't really have been returned. Ours were yellow for some strange reason – not a very 'Police' colour that. Personally, I was back on the Queensbury Gardens beat, which contrary to all expectation from our senior management hadn't 'kicked-off' in the wake of Liverpool's massive riots. I liked to think that I'd had a part to play in that through my hard work in the community. Now however, as a married man, it was becoming a time of re-appraisal for me. Risks now seemed riskier than before and I found myself thinking about possible new careers. The main impediment to this was my lack of orthodox educational qualifications. So, I was still paying the price it seemed for my eccentric attitude towards life.

Toxteth still hung over us psychologically. We used the surplus vans to patrol around on nights 'mob-handed', dropping on trouble before it could develop and snatching offenders away. A lot of the local yobs couldn't get used to the unmarked vans – they acted like 'Q cars' – deliberately disguised as harmless civilian vehicles. I remember catching one of the Patterson family, waiting patiently in a stolen car at a red traffic light. His classic response – read out in court – was:

'If I'd known that it was the Fed's yer'd never have caught me big '"G" man'.

Obviously he'd been watching too many American gangster movies…

One night I was ambling around the Town Centre near to the

main junction of Conway Street and Argyle Street. Kid Curry was out in the hire van with the Cat and three of the other lads. There was a report of a fight about a quarter of a mile along Conway Street, at a Greek Kebab house. I saw the van roar past and thought that I'd head up there to lend a hand. Conway Street is a long straight thoroughfare and it was easy to see the van pull in and the Bobbies get out to deal with the situation. As I got nearer, I could see that there were more than a dozen yobs milling around. Getting closer still, I saw the Bobbies re-embark into the van and drive off leaving at least a dozen of the now well angry yobs behind. I was at the point when I had to make a decision: do I carry on and walk towards them, or do I turn around? Well, 12 to 1 are unfavourable odds in anyone's book! So, I turned around and walked slowly back towards the junction at Argyle Street. Inevitably… I heard the sound of running feet from behind and I knew that it must be those yobs. It was better to turn and face them than simply to get myself jumped. I was surrounded… They were annoyed that one of their number had been snatched by my colleagues. I was annoyed too! It seemed to me to be a daft thing to do, leaving behind a large number of angry and aggressive yobbo's who were likely to cause even more trouble. It also had a personal slant to it as well – I mean heck this was *ME* in the middle of all this shit. That kind of predicament tends to concentrate the mind somewhat. It was one of those times when I resigned myself to getting a kicking. I tried one last 'rational' thing; that was to suggest that they all walk down to the Nick with me and we could see if we could sort things out for their mate. Crap really… if I'd have gotten them there then they'd all have ended up in the cells – and they knew it. The tension increased and it was only seconds away from detonation. I knew that I was going to get done, but I was going to take a few of these 'brave' bastards with me. At that point, a Traffic car pulled in over the other side of the road. I nodded to the driver who got out obviously realising that all was not well. That was when I got the first punch – straight in the face. As always when the odds were against me, I resorted to the Hop-Gar style – simply now out of trained instinct. It has a peculiar psychological quality – noted by many others; in that it makes you become *very* aggressive. OK you run out of steam quicker because of the larger and more powerful movements – but you stand a more immediate chance of survival against multiple attackers if you simply go 'ape' – which is precisely what I did... I was aware of the Traffic Bobby wading in with me He was a very big lad, around 6ft 4" or so and had a lot of weight to throw, which made up for his lack of numbers and technique. My radio got snatched out from its harness – a favoured yobbo's trick, but I began to make contact with the Hop-Gar hits. I was wearing leather gloves, which helped to tighten my fists and prevent injury to my hands. The cries of pain from the impact of my punches acted on the gang as a whole. They withdrew a distance, like a shoal of startled fish. I was having none of that – powered by adrenalin; I grabbed the ringleader by his throat and groin – taking him to ground and pulling violently on his testicles:

'Now...FUCKING BACK OFF OR I'LL PULL HIS BALLS OFF! ... I yelled at his mates.

Of course, they had backed off already – but that was a mere technicality...

Just then, the van returned and a number of arrests were made. I was to say the least not best pleased that they'd disappeared off in the first place, but the response was that they hadn't known that I was there. Well... true I suppose. Calming down I accepted the matter. Some weeks later I saw the ringleader again. I stopped him but he didn't recognise me – just kept saying that: *'One of your lot nearly castrated me!'*

'Really, tut-tut how inconsiderate!'

He was too pissed to remember who I was – but the event and his wounded manhood had stayed 'firmly' in his mind. In the court case that followed, he pointed at me plaintively and said:

'That bastard grabbed me sack yer honour!' His honour reflected for a moment and then pronounced the technique: *'Most appropriate!'*

Afterwards, I was aware that Ho-Sing's Mantis style hadn't featured at all in the fight. Only my old all time favourite Hop-Gar Lion's Roar. Thinking about this, it was obvious that as yet I hadn't made the Mantis my own. Also, Hop-Gar had the edge in my estimation in the kind of situation that I'd been in. So, I was still struggling to solve the 'form versus function' problem with respect to the Mantis, when I had the good fortune to see a televised lecture on the psychology and physiology of perception by the Oxford Professor Colin Blakemore. This was one of those magic moments in life when a door to understanding opens and takes you beyond the problem. Professor Blakemore isn't a martial artist, but he was concerned with the brain and how much information it needed to make sense of such things as pattern recognition and movement. Both of course being vital in a fight. He gave a demonstration involving two people dressed all in black moving about in a normally lit room. Obviously they could both be seen clearly – and the brain made appropriate and contextual sense of what it could 'see'. Then, the lights were switched off, and the people of course disappeared into the darkness. The brain could see nothing – so it was as if nothing was there. Suddenly however, a series of tiny lights appeared which were moving about in a chaotic way. At first it wasn't clear what was going on – but when the lights stopped moving, a clear impression of two human figures could be seen. The viewers only visual information was a series of twelve lights, situated one on each ankle, knee, hip, wrist, elbow and shoulder. But, that was sufficient for the brain to begin to fill in the gaps!

Then when the lights moved again, it was easy to 'plot' and follow the movements. This clearly illustrated how little information was actually needed to pick out the shape and movement dynamics of a human being! Wow! That suggested

Torso

Clock

& Limb

Control

Points

that was all you need in a fight; a simple model to overlay on any movement at all, with the minimum of fuss and confusion! Hmmm… back to the Mantis…. The classical Southern Mantis style of Kung-Fu has a similar-ish system, in that it considers the human body to be made up of 'three hands' the 'Sam-Gwan' of Kung-Fu. The first hand extends from the fingers to the wrist. The second from the wrist to the elbow, and the third represents the rest of the body as a whole unit but with the power delivered through the shoulder. These are considered as sources of power in a traditional sense. I'd always accepted traditional explanations in their own terms, but had also gone to western physics, mechanics and leverage principles for a more concise and perhaps elegant understanding. Maybe if I re-styled the Sam-Gwan according to those lights on the arms? Maybe the legs should be included too, as separate limbs with separate control points? Maybe that's what the Sam-Gwan should or at least could be – elegant and simple control points! Watching Ho-Sing again closely, he hit the shoulders, controlled the elbow – a familiar Mantis technique called Huen Juang or to 'follow the elbow'. He also controlled the wrist, thereby isolating action to the two other arm joints – then controlling them as necessary.

There it was! Blakemore's model in action even if by another name or as in this case, by no name at all. Wing-Chun Kung-Fu works on an arm controlling principle too. However, it mainly – not exclusively – but mainly, controls along the forearms between the wrist and elbow. Seldom does it pass up above the elbow and very rarely does it control the shoulder. Ho-Singseemed to be the opposite – the elbow always, and the shoulder if possible. Maybe then Ho-Sing had an internal model in his brain – like a computer – on how to plot intercept and destroy an attack. He wouldn't have to know this consciously for it to happen. It could work simply through the years of experience and learning that had gone into his art. Eddie too, his closest and in my opinion most skilled student did similar things. They communicated outside of normal language by a kind of resonance or rapport, so no wordy explanation was necessary between them.

Control

Planes

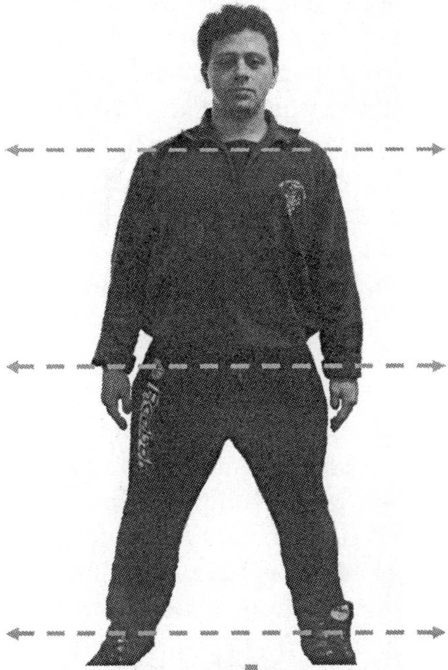

Being me however, I decided to see if a conscious knowledge of the way the brain works with its perceptual information could improve things. My own 'model' was therefore at an early stage of development – some things needed adding, but I was confident that in time and with the pressure testing I was getting in the Police – that they would become clear to me in due course. Two quite unrelated things then happened that provided me with the inspiration and indeed the keys, to develop the missing pieces. After 7 years in the job, I was belatedly allocated to a police driving course –without which you were not allowed to drive police vehicles. The courses were run from Smithdown Lane 'Garage' in Liverpool, and involved initially a five-week intensive course with one instructor and three 'crew' assigned to each vehicle. The discipline was strict as Merseyside Police Driving School prides itself on being one of the very best in the country. There are fundamental Home-Office standards that must be met with by all police driving schools, but Merseyside exceeded them, and by some at that. The vehicles were valeted by us each morning, and then taken out for a series of tutored drives around the country. The police have an interesting 'System' of car-control, which involves a six-featured process of assessment of any and of all driving scenario's. It is difficult to learn at first as it requires the elimination of unnecessary actions and the training of road perceptions to a refined art. Skidpan training, high-speed manoeuvres, night driving, road-craft theory, and vehicle mechanical theory, all played their part. We were constantly being pressure-tested over our ability to respond according to the 'System'. Criticism was intense, from peers as well as the instructor. And we had to pass independent assessment of our skills on the public road; over road obstacles courses, manoeuvring, on the skidpan and by theoretical examination.

In Merseyside at that time, driving courses were graded according to 'Class'. My training was a 'Standard Car Course' and a pass was possible at either Class Three or Class Four. Class Four – the minimum, was equivalent to the UK Civilian

Advanced Driving qualification from the Institute for Advanced Motorists (IAM) and The Royal Society for the Prevention of Accidents (RoSPA) Advanced Drivers Association. Incidentally, the examiners for both of those organisations are Police Class One drivers. The same system is used on all police driving courses, the difference in class comes with skill, polish, and further pressure testing. It can seem a robotic like way of processing information – at first, but it produces confident drivers who are very safe to drive at high speed under all road conditions. The System itself was developed in the 1930's and despite advances in vehicle technology it still stands proud as the best system anywhere for public road driving. The reason? It is systematic and based upon the natural progression of information processing that occurs in the brain. This eliminates or reduces error and allows for safe and timely correction. Driving, like combat, is a sensory rich environment with plenty of opportunities to get yourself hurt or killed. Things happen very suddenly and from all directions. Being able to sift and sort minimal sensory information is vital. The 'System' really shines under extreme pressure at very high speed on dangerous public roads. Nothing has been developed that can beat it.

Hmmm… Just the kind of thing that was needed for a new model of combat information processing! That thought went into incubation as other things sifted and sorted themselves around for future use.

Well, I passed the course with a Class Three – good enough for Panda's, personnel carriers and prison vans. Returning back to my Section I was given the chance to drive the Town Centre Panda (the Maroon Buffoon's Panda, he was temporarily on the Rock Ferry car) on rotation with my Queensbury Gardens foot beat. 'Golf Mike 32' as it was now called was the busiest Panda at the busiest 'Bridewell Station' anywhere in the UK outside of central London according to Police statistics. Tear-arsing around became a fun thing. Ignoring traffic signals at will, speed limits exceeded as the need required, high-speed chases and scrambles to your mates in trouble –wonderful! I liked to practice hand-brake turns on the Asda car park in Conway Street. It had a 'ski slope' style ramp off its roof down to a huge undulating tarmac-surfaced parking space: which was ideal for practicing the finer points of car control; especially in winter! Panda's unlike the Traffic and the Fast Response vehicles, were essentially very ordinary cars that you had to screw to get any performance out of. Consequently, we were always 'chasing the rev's'. And, it is true that skill makes a difference as does local knowledge when it comes to car chases. Indeed I'd argue that you need more demonstrative skill to 'Panda' successfully than you do to drive Traffic vehicles. Panda's lacked many of the things that make driving easy so you had to be good to get by. Many times we caught much higher-powered cars simply by taking the Panda to the very limit of its performance: engine and handling wise. Without our training though we'd have all been killed in the first week, no doubt about it.

I'd decided to formalise my psychology studies with the Open University and signed on for one of their honours degree courses. This would help in three distinct ways: Firstly, it would allow me to ground all of my many and varied branches of private study into something formally recognised as an academic discipline. This included my personal development – a kind of on-going self-analysis that had been continuing in depth and in detail since I was sixteen and in a less structured way since I was a child. Secondly, it would give me a perspective on the East outside of its influence, so that I could assess some of the more esoteric aspects of Traditional Chinese Martial Arts rationally. Finally, psychology as an experimental discipline, included the study of perceptual processes including early research on combat information processing in World War II fighter pilots. All in all… ideal!

I had consulted with both Master Ho-Sing and Master Chan on my Toxteth experiences, hoping to get something back that would help. They did their best but it was clearly outside of their range of experience. They were both accomplished street fighters, but Toxteth was the biggest fight *ever* in the UK short of an actual war. Master Chan knew by now that we had gone over to Ho-Sing, but he was forgiving in mood. He asked me to accept an Honorary Presidents post for his school, now approaching its fifth anniversary. I accepted and attended the celebrations. I noted how few of the 'old guard' were left. Even many of the Chinese had gone, leaving the remnants of the first generation and some up and coming people to fill in the gaps. By now I was entering a kind of 'Wilderness phase' with respect to my martial arts training. I was gripped by the possibilities of developing a science of personal combat – applicable to any martial art, and I was getting all the pressure-testing that I could ask for with respect to trying the new model out. The rigmarole of class training with a group of less experienced students had lost all of its appeal. I now decided that a 'consultancy' with highly skilled Masters was the best approach for me I saw Ho-Sing, Master Chan and Ken and Philip Liu, all good fighters and all experienced men. I trained with Eddie who's natural intelligence for the street helped enormously as did his guidance over the Mantis.

Meanwhile, we'd got ourselves a new Sergeant. Chris Garvey was still Station Sergeant. Townson (sadly) still one of the two Patrol Sergeants. This new fellow however seemed a very odd character, and at first I thought that we'd get on extremely well. He was an ex Regional Crime Squad Detective Sergeant, who had passed his promotion examination to Inspector and now needed some uniform experience for his promotion prospects to be secured. Tommy Johnson was a laid back, but very keen minded fellow, who'd developed a style of playing the fool to get people off-guard. It was so effective in criminal investigations that he had earned the nick-name 'Columbo' after the fictional American Detective. Indeed so similar was he, even down to the dirty raincoat, that some suspected that it was a deliberately crafted persona.

The Falkland's War was in full swing and like most people in the UK we followed its progress closely – thinking very much about what the servicemen and Women were going through down in the South Atlantic. Cruising around one evening, checking some industrial property, I came across a warehouse unit on a trading estate with a hole in its wall. Clearly, thieves had entered by knocking the bricks out. The premises appeared to be alarmed but there was sign on the building to denote either its ownership or purpose. I radioed in my findings and the Control Room confirmed that there was no listed key-holder. I thought that I'd better check things out, so I went in through the burglars access point. Inside, I got a hell of a surprise. All around were work-benches with electronic parts spread out – and along one wall – racks of torpedoes! They were red in colour and marked 'MK 24 Tigerfish'. I knew enough to realise that these were the Navy's latest and most secret acquisition. The alarm control box had been forced and deactivated - expertly! Columbo turned up – his usual persona in place:

'Hello Steve, nothing much goin' on here really, just a warehouse. The thieves probably didn't know what was inside and have buggered off disappointed'. I hated being patronised:

'What about the War Sarge, what about those Mk 24 Tigerfish torpedo's? Maybe this is something more than yer average burglary, that alarm system has been expertly b-ypassed !'

'Nah, leave it alone, I'll get someone out to secure the premises'.

'What about a report?'

'Leave it Steve, leave it'.

Columbo didn't leave it, he wasn't seen again for ages but his radio traffic was very busy. His car was there hours later along with some unfamiliar vehicles. It seems that Special Branch became involved, and a certain Sergeant in all likelihood took the credit for the discovery. I didn't like being fobbed off, but at least our Section Inspector Dave Williams acknowledged that it was a 'good find'. Indeed of all my Inspectors –throughout the whole of my service I got on with him the best. He was a law graduate and an experienced policeman and I felt a lot of mutual respect between us. With Columbo though, things went from bad to worse. Townson, as he had before with other Sergeants, got his three pennies worth in and engendered a certain attitude towards me from Columbo. That misunderstanding was to last some years. Columbo didn't like the idea that I was doing the Open University and took every opportunity to mock it towards my coleauges. He didn't believe in the Queensbury Gardens scheme either and again did his best to undermine that too. Fortunately, I had Inspector Williams full support in that regard, so he was limited with respect to the damage that he could do. Politics aside, I was getting some learning experiences in fighting wise…

'Bad Guy's' was an aptly named dive of a night club situated in the lower part of Conway Street. Trouble there was frequent, but, there was also a good relationship overall between the staff and the police. This was helped by the willingness of the management to provide 'refreshments' both to uniform and CID personnel. The bouncers were a mixed bunch, not of the quality of those to be found say at Rupert's or Sir James' Clubs.

One night, trouble had flared and the police had been called (me actually). I was not one to frequent Bad Guy's under normal circumstances so I was an unfamiliar face. A dispute had arisen between some 'punters' and the doormen. It seemed to me that the doormen were in the wrong and I said so openly. They were not amused. Obviously used to getting the back-up of the police without question – the doorman at the centre of the dispute became quite besides himself:

'What the fuckin hell are you doin' eh? We give you bastards all the booze and grub yer want and you do this to us!'

'Sorry pal I don't know you and I don't know what your talking

about. I'm here as a result of your call and it seems to me that the lady has a point about your behaviour'.

*'Shit, you fuckin twat – do you know Inspector ******* eh? Well, he gets pissed here on duty all the fuckin time, we've even got it on film! Sort that bitch out and fuck off!'*

I decided that appearing "non-threatening" was a good move, so… I put my hands in my pockets and smiled at him…

As I flew through the air, I wondered at how cartoon like things had suddenly become. I remember hitting the wall and sliding down, like the unfortunate cat in the Tom and Jerry show. I got up dazed but still sufficiently aware of what was in front of me. The bouncer was white faced and shaking his fist. The women on whose behalf I'd made the point of criticising this fellow in the first place were screaming, other bouncers tried to restrain him, but he wrestled with them and then made off out of the door.

I ran after him, passing a 'Scramble' message down the radio. Outside, he stopped and turned towards me as if to give up. I stopped too but at an appropriate distance. I could tell from his eyes that he would hit again if I stepped closer. He started to step back again, so I matched his distance- he half stepped once more and I closed the gap with a forward step that penetrated directly into his centre line – just as his weight was transferring to his back foot. He tried to kick with his lead leg – which is what I wanted because his weight was going in the opposite direction of his blow. I kick-blocked his leg on the calf muscle – twisting with my foot to open him out. He lost balance and fell forward – arms grasping for my head. I kept up my forward momentum – and punched him on the sternum, at which point he literally 'sat down' on the pavement and threw up. That was that – no more fight left in him. Helpfully, the Maroon Buffoon arrived and our man was cuffed and arrested. He was charged with assault occasioning Actual Bodily Harm (ABH). Thinking back, I was pleased enough with my performance *after* being hit, but before hand oh…no… I mean, putting my hands in my pocket and smiling. Well, I'd never do that again with a bouncer… would I?

By the next shift on Nights I was feeling a little better about myself. My pride was hit every bit as hard as my cheekbone by that bouncer. Fortunately, he hadn't caught me on the chin. I was on foot patrol outside Victoria Court, a block of flats no less notorious than Queensbury Gardens itself. It was 'kicking-out-time' from the pubs, but the 'Sea-Dog' public house showed no sign of letting up on its trade. Turning a wisely blind eye I walked on, wondering what the night would bring. There was always the thought of the unexpected to keep you from getting bored. Lost in such thoughts, I suddenly became aware of shouting and of two figures running hell for leather towards the pub. The first one – who was obviously being chased crashed through the doors, the other an older and much bigger man cursed and kicked at them:

'Whoa , steady on mate what's going on?'

'That little shit robbed me car'.

'You saw him?'

'Fuckin right I fuckin saw him!'

'Where's your car now?'

'At work, I'm a doorman. The cheeky bastard drove it from me house to the fuckin club were I work!'

Hmmm… *'So, you've got the car back then?'*

'That's not it is it! That's not the fuckin point!'

'No, no of course not, I'm just getting the facts straight'.

Anyway, it turned out that he knew the lad concerned, Paul Doughty, one of another hard-case family in the Town Centre. He was adamant that he wanted him charged. So, I went into the pub and affected a search. Doughty saw me and made a run for it. I caught him and he put up a struggle. I ended up chinning him with an elbow to stop him kicking the hell out of me. The bouncer didn't get involved –probably wisely, but he gave a statement of evidence to support a charge against Doughty of Assault on Police, in addition to the charge of 'Unlawful Taking of a Motor Vehicle'. Doughty, being Doughty pleaded not guilty and the job was referred to the Crown Court for trial.

Later that week, the Maroon Buffoon and I were doubled up on GM 31 when we got a call to go to attend at a violent domestic dispute. Routine enough… On arrival, the street was full of people – neighbours. The door to the house in question was open and sounds of screaming were coming from inside:

'Get in there he's murderin' his wife and kid's!' said a female neighbour.

We went in to an upstairs front bedroom. Inside I saw a woman huddled up with her children in a corner. Then, standing upright on the bed – was a *very* angry man:

'Fuckin get out!'

'I'm sorry we can't do that until you've calmed down'.

'FUCKIN GET OUT!'

'I'm concerned for the safety of you wife and children, I have to stay until this is sorted out'.

'THIS IS YOUR LAST FUCKIN CHANCE!!!'

Well, he did warn me didn't he… You know how it is, you've made a mistake but somehow you just go and do it again. I put my hands into my pockets and smiled at him, to show that I wasn't threatening him. A feeling of de-ja vu occurred to me as I flew through the air and slid down the wall like the unfortunate cat Tom, in the Tom and Jerry cartoon show. The Maroon Buffoon excelled himself. as I was trying to make sure that I was still in this world, he lunged across at the mans legs and rugby tackled him – with such force that the fellow fell forwards base over apex, straight off the bed.

By now I was fully 'compos mentis' and drew my handcuffs. It was then that I realised who our man was; he was the bouncer who'd had his car stolen by Doughty! That produced the weird state of affairs wherein he was witness for the prosecution on an assault charge in one Crown Court job, only to be the defendant in another. In both sets of proceedings I was the aggrieved party!

It was the hardest hit I'd taken up to that time - anywhere. And at last I got the point. Fate had been kind to me. It could have been oh so much worse. The bouncer ended up paying £50.00 in compensation to me as well as being convicted of the assault. Fifty quid – shit I mean he could have killed me! Ah well… At least the Maroon Buffoon had redeemed himself. He was a 'sound' fellow at heart and a hell of a lot more experienced than me in the job. I couldn't help but like him, and I still miss him even to this day… sort of….

My studies with the Open University were helping enormously in understanding the role of perception in combat. The World War II study had focussed on the differences perceptually between air combat fighter aces and more mediocre pilots. The difference seemed to be in the way the aces were able to model the shape and movement dynamics of an enemy aircraft and their ability to anticipate what an aircraft could do simply by being an aircraft. This involved an empathy or rapport with the enemy pilot – 'second guessing' them – accurately. It was obvious that it was not only perception –as in what you saw or felt that was important, but also an internal mental map or model of the situation as a whole.

I added this to a deep reflection on the processes involved in the Police's 'six featured system of car control'. This number six was significant too, as experimental psychologists had discovered a magic number of '7 plus or minus 2' for the number of chunked items the brain could efficiently deal with in its short term working memory – say for example over the time taken to compute a complex driving or combat flying situation. I then devised a similar, linear, seven featured combat system – designed just as in the Police driving case, for each feature to be considered 'in sequence' rapidly in any hazardous situation:

1. PERCEPTION: the actual detection of a threat or situation is necessary before we can do anything about it, so this feature must occur first.

2. TARGETING: the 'shape' of the attack – identifying what you are up against.

3. RANGE: the distance to the target and whether that distance is opening, closing or varying. Is it a non-contact or contact distance?

.4. ENGAGEMENT: contact with the threat as appropriately targeted and ranged. The Chinese call this 'making the bridge'.

5. SPEED: the correct speed of interception/attack is vital as over-gearing can make you miss or be otherwise blocked. Speed includes timing therefore as well as physical A to B velocity.

6. POWER: impact force can come from speed as in the formula force (f) equals mass (m) times acceleration (a) $f = ma$. However, features 1 through 4 above also have a contribution as lower velocity hits on vulnerable areas have great stopping power. Small striking surfaces such as single knuckle hits to

pressure points, or large area sensory nerve stimulation (as in a loose and stinging slap) impart different but useable amounts of force, and therefore power.

7. DESTRUCTION: the end goal of features 1 through 6. All actions are intended to lead towards the destruction of the opponents attack or of the attacker (as appropriate), as a threat. The psychological aspects of destruction are important too, as an attacker can be destroyed 'mentally' even if relative unharmed physically.

My police experience at the Driving School had shown that such rapid and linear calculation was not easy at first, but when it had become automatic then it promoted a cool head under pressure and smooth progressive action.

My psychology studies had shown that the expertly trained human brain quite literally builds a 'Battle Computer' to take it through combat.

So, how about doing that consciously – and then pressure testing it?

Looking back over my by now many years of fighting – right up from those brawling street fights as a seven year old, it seemed to me that the most important thing was to be able to 'shape' an attacker. Perception, should of course come first in an ideal world, but suppose you get jumped or cannot 'see' or otherwise clearly perceive what the hell was going on?

Well, given that most people are attacked by other people, I reasoned that a simple as possible a model of the human form was the logical starting point. This, was the familiar 'pin man' and of course it linked well with Professor Blakemore's 'illuminated limb joints' demonstration.

Hmmm…well, suppose you are at such close range that you

only have a view of the persons' torso – rather than the limbs

The Battle Computer's linear processing combat programme:

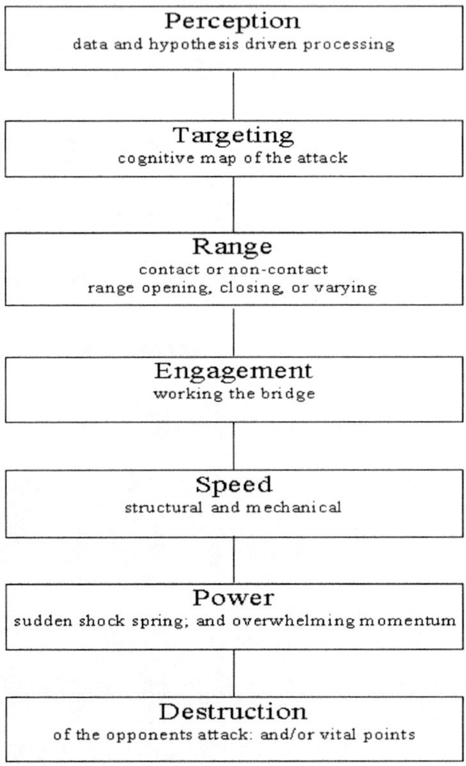

what then?

To answer this, I reflected on the basic shape of the human body minus its limbs (including as a special consideration; the head). It seemed to me to be roughly circular, with the limbs, head and groin 'attaching' at cardinal points – as on a clock face. So, I assigned a clock number to each shoulder, each hip, the head and the groin:

Right shoulder = 11 o'clock.

Head and neck region = 12 o'clock.
Left shoulder = 1 o'clock.

Left hip = 5 o'clock.

Groin area = 6 o'clock.

Right hip = 7 o'clock.

The centre of mass of the body, the solar-plexus region, was also at the centre point of the 'clock face'. This would be the point at which the hands of the clock attached, and it turned out – the point from which all other clock face points were roughly equidistant from one another.

So, up close and personal, you wouldn't have to be able to 'see' your opponent all that clearly – *if* your battle-computers programming allowed computation of relative spatial position of these points you could then hit or control them at will.
As for the limbs?

Well, they were dealt with by their major control points sited on the three main joints (as outlined earlier on). Also, for 'blind control' – once you had contact with an attackers arm – his head was *always* at the end of it –along its line so to speak. The same being true of the groin, it always lies at the end point of the leg, not matter how the leg is positioned or is moving. Not forgetting of course the head, as the command and control centre. The head is effectively a fifth limb and used as a weapon in itself as in butting or biting.

Hmmm…

The last thing that was added was the concept of 'control planes'. At very close contact range – grappling comes into play

– quite naturally. Here, balance is the fundamental thing – keeping yours and compromising the other fellows'. In an upright position, perpendicular to the ground, it seemed that three fundamental control planes crossed the body. These I termed *transverse control planes*:

1. Transverse shoulder plane: running from one shoulder through the neck and throat region onto the other shoulder. If this can be controlled, you can stop yourself being punched or kicked at close range. It also facilitates headlock and take-down manoeuvres and allows the opponent to be 'spun' on their axis with small contact hits using the palm, forearm and elbow etc.

2. Transverse hip plane: running from one hip through the groin area to the other hip. Again at close range it can be used to stop yourself from being kicked. It can also open up take-down or pressure point strike opportunities.

3. Transverse support plane; running through both ankles – if both feet are on the floor. This describes the 'stance' taken by the target. The narrowest upright support plane is one foot on the ground. Attacking this by striking at the ankles, foot sweeps, foot treads and leg-trapping techniques, will compromise balance and prevent mobility and kicking by the target.

Then, a final vertical control plane:

4. Median control plane: this runs vertically rather than horizontally, and in an upright person passes directly down through numbers 12 and 6 on the body-clock – terminating on the floor at the targets centre of balance.
On the ground the control planes work with the body clock and limb control points to isolate, control and engage different parts of the target.

Grapplers do this almost naturally, the control points being 'factored in' on the basis of real 'in the dirt' scrapping experience. What's different about my approach is that it's reduced to simple elements that work equally as well whether you're standing up and slugging it out, or wallowing around on the floor. I reckon it's the lack of full-bodied close contact in many of the so-called 'striking arts' (e.g. traditional Karate) that makes many of their practitioners seem so weak when they've been taken to the floor in a fight. The reverse is sometimes true of grapplers, they often lack sophistication in the striking dimension of fighting and literally wade in without enough thought, only to be picked off by elegant 'anti-grappling' techniques.

Surely what's needed is a simple information processing model that doesn't really distinguish between what are popularly called 'ranges' in interpersonal combat, but instead works 'holistically'. The range to technique classification has always been troublesome for me. It was made popular following the death of Bruce Lee by some of his students who in quoting Lee's theories claimed that man-on-man fighting can be described according to the following four ranges:

KickingRange
BoxingRange
TrappingRange
GrapplingRange

(going from furthest away to the closest).

All very neat but not at all accurate: quite misleading in fact. The first problem is that 'distance' is classified according to categories of *technique*. Well, distance has been measured abstractly many times in the past. For example, in medieval times it was common to ask: *'How far to the next village?'* only to receive the reply *'Five bow shots'*.

Hmmm…

What kind of bow? A longbow, shortbow, crossbow, composite bow etc etc. Not very precise is it! It's the same with measuring distance according to the physical techniques in the martial arts. As anyone with a brain could work out, it's possible to be either kicked, punched or grappled from any of those supposed magic four ranges.

These 'technique equals range' errors actually describe a phenomenon that is far more subtle and far more useful: range is a physical distance – a spatial relationship between two or more points *relative* to one another. 'Length' is a single dimension, so too is breadth and depth. Together they make the familiar three physical dimensions of space. Try as we might, we cannot actually experience physical reality in any *single* dimension, our brains simply aren't wired up that way. Why? Because the physical, spatial world, is three-dimensional and that is what our species has evolved to deal with in everyday life.

So, the four ranges mentioned above are more like 'dimensions' than true ranges. There is a dimension of combat that involves mainly hand techniques such as striking, there is a dimension that describes what could be broadly called kicking methods and yet another that describes grappling. These make up the three fundamental physical dimensions of combat. And just as with length, breadth and depth, they tend to occur together as one composite whole. There are other 'dimensions' of course than just simply the physical. There is the 'temporal' dimension (time) as in speed and timing – taken as an interactive factor with the opponents position or movement. Then, the most problematic of all, that of psychology: the effects of learning, instinct, conditioning and even psychological suggestion. Many fights are won and lost in this transcendent dimension alone.

In its simplest terms there are only two 'ranges'; non-contact and contact. In the street, if you are very lucky, things will 'kick off' (metaphorically!) from the first range: non-contact. At least that way you may have a chance, even if that means acting pre-emptively. If the fight starts at physical contact range, then the momentum of your opponent may simply overwhelm you. If you last long enough to recover some balance and clarity then you'd better regain the initiative, and that's were the battle computer with the torso clock, control points and planes model comes into its own.

In terms of 'imagery training' I found it useful to visualise clear sheets of acetate with the clock, planes and control points, overlain onto a pin man representation of a human target – and then think about nothing else – just pick everything off accordingly. It would be a simple thing to actually generate graphically on a computer, effectively producing a 'HUD' a 'Head Up Display' the kind of thing the pilots of jet fighters and helicopter gun-ships use in stressful air combat environments. I am involved in developing just such a training project at this moment so watch this space!

The last advantage of this combat model is that it allows the easy and natural spot location of vital and pressure points on the target. If you can find a control point or control a transverse plane, you can reach the pressure points that lie close by. All in all it is a relatively simple system that is independent of style, and one that has the advantage of being led by *principles* rather than the limiting dogmatic edict of any given martial arts system.

In its development it is a thoroughly western model, grounded in science, logic and hard physical pressure testing. When applied to oriental (or indeed Western) martial arts styles, it transcends culture and becomes a universal framework therefore, for the delivery of *any* combat system.

The last major development in 1982 concerned my wish to get some practical experience to back-up my psychology degree studies. Using contacts at Serve Wirral, I was put in touch with a Mrs Molly Dobson, at the newly built Arrowe Park Hospital. Molly was nominally a psychiatric social worker, but her training and remit was extended to psychotherapy with psychiatric out-patients. After an interview with her, she introduced me to Professor F. J. Roberts of Liverpool University. He was the chief psychiatrist for the Wirral Area Health Authority. He agreed to me serving a part time apprentiship with Mrs Dobson. So, I began at last to work with people who suffered as Carl Jung had put it from 'sickness of the Soul'. This combined with my work with John Cain broadened even my police experiences out.

Naturally enough there was yet more bemusement and indeed some frank suspicion from my coleauges in the Police – but I didn't give a dam. My life's trajectory had been to study and hopefully to understand human nature – and the mental health and healing fields were a living laboratory of the human condition unfettered or disguised by rank, status or occupation.

1983 brought a brief television moment of fame for Pauline. She had been working in the Civil Service in the Department of Employment since leaving school. The independent television programme 'World in Action', decided to do a programme about the conditions of poverty and social depravation in the Birkenhead area called 'On The Scrap Heap'. It's focus was a group of unemployed Birkenhead men, who it was claimed had to literally scratch for a living by foraging around on Bidston Local Authority Rubbish Tip.

Pauline was the unwilling Unemployment Clerk filmed with a secret camera after the TV company had been refused access to shoot a scene with one of the men signing on as unemployed. She'd got a lot of unwanted attention following her appearance years earlier on BBC TV's 'Jim 'LL Fix It' and now a similar thing happened with her being followed from work by unsavoury types. On the last occasion, I was there to sort it out, as she walked across Hamilton Square towards the Nick. He saw me coming and ran – which is fortunate for all concerned because a threat to Pauline was the ultimate sin in my book and if I'd have got near to him I would have impaled the bastard on the nearest railings.

We dealt with the same people at our respective places of work, and any connection between the two of us by the local yobs would have meant trouble for her, but this was too much.

She'd put up with me working shifts since she'd known me, but now married and alone at home for hours on end, things were getting her down. Her Mother had cut me off altogether since the wedding, not speaking to me at all – it was as if I were invisible – meanwhile fawning all over Pauline in a sickly way. She wouldn't even acknowledge our home – never visiting it. In public she would try to introduce Pauline now a married woman as her 'baby'. Naturally this was rejected, but she knew Pauline was vulnerable and she exploited it to the full. Her Father was little different, and her Sister Claire would call to see her when I was at work and try to undermine her and make her feel unhappy with her lot in life. Neither Marie nor Claire were happy and they couldn't it seems stand to see Pauline in a loving and stable relationship. Still, it would take much more than that to shake our relationship – and they never succeeded.

Meanwhile at work, Columbo was appearing to be even more 'strange in manner'. Maybe the last straw for him was my working at the hospital part-time:

'There just isn't any dock yer can lose me in yer know'.

'Eh!'

'I know what yer about, and I'm tellin' yer it won't work on me!'.

'What? I don't know what you mean?'

'You think yer clever don't yer, well, I've been in this job fer years an' I've seen it all. I can make it very difficult for yer, just you remember that!' And with that, he was gone…! Hmmm… a little bit of paranoia there perhaps…?

Still, someone must have appreciated me. I got an invitation to lecture at Mather Avenue on 'successful community policing' to new recruits. I was even given a Panda to drive over there – and paid either overtime or given time-off from shift duty to attend. It was a great success, mainly I believe because I was straight about things. I told the recruits how to survive in an inner city community and what had gone wrong in Toxteth. That probably irked Columbo too – out of all the community beat officers in the force – it was me who was selected. It seemed that my working of the Queensbury Gardens Project was seen as 'exemplary'.

Not that that stopped me getting into trouble of course…

One night I was doubled-up with Kid Curry on the 'Oxton Panda' – GM34. This was the quietest of the Town's cars and that allowed a certain licence to roam around poaching on the other Panda's beats. There had been a periodic IRA scare and we had all been extra vigilant – just in case. As Bobbies will when they feel psychologically threatened, Kidd Curry decided to check out the details of any local IRA sympathisers or suspects. He found one, who lived in Rock Ferry. I was surprised, I knew the fellow and he seemed harmless enough, not bright just a minor thief.

Kid Curry had other ideas:

'That buggers probably handling semtex, and I'll bet he's armed. He rides a motor-bike yer know Steve. I've clocked him around Birkenhead Park. I think we should wait for him and give him a once-over search'.

I laughed thinking that this sounded typical 'Curry' – hyperbole and promises!

Well, the Kid was driving, so I had to kinda go along with it. Sure enough we saw our man; Sean MacNamara. He was speeding along Park Road North in the general direction of

Queensbury Gardens: *'Hmm…Never seen him round my patch before Kid, wonder what he's up to?'*

'No good yer can bet! – come 'ead let's pull 'im'.

As we caught up, we could see a bag containing an 'L' shaped object dangling from his handlebars:

'It's a fuckin gun!' Screamed the Kid. *'I fuckin new it!'*

He accelerated hard and aimed the Panda at McNamara's rear wheel as if to tip him off. At that point MacNamara became aware of us, and looking over his shoulder roared off at full speed towards the Tower block flats. Kid Curry roared after him eyes bulging, 'red-mist' in full bloom. Inside the maisonette area of Queensbury Gardens we caught up with him. McNamara was standing behind his bike – now parked and mounted on its stand.

We got out of the Panda – bonnet facing him and headlights full on. I started to remember Leroy Brown and his Bentley – and began to wish that I was somewhere else:
'What's in the bag then Mac?' asked the Kid.

MacNamara reached down for it… and the Kid jumped back.

There was a silent pause as McNamara slowly pulled out… a wheel brace for his motor-bike….

My new combat system was at last making the Mantis Kung-Fu style work very well for me. It is a style that favours pressure point hits and close quarter control and so they dovetailed perfectly. I was also thinking a lot about the consequences of belting a member of the public a bit too hard. I'd seen the result of one man being hit too hard in a street fight outside the Fireman's Arms pub in Birkenhead – he'd died from the secondary impact of his head on the floor, so knocking someone out cold wasn't always the best option. Pressure point stop-hits processed through the combat system seemed to be a good option. But, the skills would have to be well trained and refined. Just as in police driver training, it takes time for the method to become a part of you and to work smoothly. Training with partners supplemented by imagery training helps but you must be able to do it for real when things kick off.

One night I was in company with a very tough colleague: Colin Peters, an ex-paratrooper and boxer. He had kept himself fit and wasn't unduly put out at the prospect of anything that he was likely to encounter on the streets. This particular night we got involved in a car chase around the Town Centre eventually ending with the suspect vehicle running off the road at the junction of Livingstone Street and Cleveland Street. The driver did a runner and Colin was out and on our man like a whippet pulling him to the ground and assuming the 'mount position' - effectively seated astride his prone prisoner. This fellow decided however that he was going to get away and a struggle ensued. Colin being the kind of chap he was; I thought that unless he got into difficulties, I'd leave him alone. The prisoner started to land some effective blows almost tipping Colin off him. Colin raised himself up and dropped a full-blooded right hook onto his jaw. As I watched the prisoner grinned and said:

'Is that the best you can fucking do?' Your nose is going to go yer twat'.

And with that he shook Colin off and started head butting at him ferociously.

It was time to intervene. I waded in from the prisoners blind side and started a stream of pressure point hit strikes, compounded with control point hits. He writhed like he was being machine gunned, lost his balance and fell – at which point Colin was on him again belting away! He was locked up and charged, with drunk driving and assault on police. Still it proved that provided I could close the gap safely between me and my target (from non-contact to contact range) then he could be drilled and dropped without the need for a potentially dangerous 'big hit' option.

On the last night of that shift, I backed the Cat up at a report of a sudden death in Prenton. Sudden Puddin's are never easy as there is always the end of someone's life to consider and the feelings of the relatives too. This one though had something of the comedic about it and shamefully we were unable to hold back on our amusement.

On arrival the house was a very large Edwardian terrace, nicely decorated and clean throughout. It was occupied by a man in his thirties and… the deceased –his Father. Going in I could hear howls of laughter from upstairs followed by silence then crying and laughter once more! Odd!

Walking into the main bedroom I saw the Cat and the Son. The Cat was trying to hold back his mirth, and the son was pacing up and down moaning.

I looked around and saw another man lying on the bed. He was fully clothed, lying on his side, head propped up on his arm apparently reading a book:

'Hello, good evening' I said to him. *'where's the deceased?'*

Howls of laughter from the Cat alerted me that I'd made a major faux pas of some kind.

The son wailed, and then laughed himself, uncontrollably. The Cat slunk out of the room choking and snorting on his now ill-repressed amusement.

I turned to the other man to ask him about the deceased, when I noticed that his mouth seemed a little more widely open than before. Perhaps he'd read something shocking in his book?

More than that he seemed quite remarkably distracted, his eyes having that far away and 'still' look to them.

As the son came back in it all dawned upon me:

'He's dead!' I exclaimed.

More cries from the son and howls of uncontrollable laughter from the Cat out on the landing – then all three of us laughed hysterically –tears running down our faces.

As the deceased face grew more and more aghast in the rigours of death, we three struggled valiantly to take the proceedings seriously and to obtain the required details for the coroner:

'Would you like a cup of tea lad's' said the son…

'If he's having one', said the Cat gesturing to Dad.

More uncontrollable laughter, as it gradually deteriorated into an impromptu 'Wake'.

An ambulance crew attended just to be sure that he was dead, and to take him to Arrowe Park to be certified. By now though Dad was in advanced rigor mortis and was about to swallow his book, so it was a just a bit obvious. The ambulance-men having missed the earlier banter couldn't understand, but as soon as 'Dad the Stiff' was moved, head still propped up on his left arm – all the tears came flooding back in the Son.

I couldn't stand the surreal atmosphere any longer – I buggered off and left the Cat to it!

The Cat could be quite unforgiving of adversity in a fellow human being, even a harmless and aggrieved member of the public. One Sunday morning it was pissing down with rain, one of those 'wall of water' jobs, so heavy that visibility was effectively zero. I was driving the GM 32 Panda and had picked the Cat up just in time for him to avoid a drenching. His aversion to getting wet matching that of his feline namesakes.

It was pointless trying to drive any further so I parked up on a piece of waste ground by the docks. Suddenly, the shape of a figure approached, looking like a drowned rat.

The Cat wound the car window down (a fraction) to reveal the face of an elderly man, the rain bouncing mercilessly on his drum-skin like bald head, despair etched into his weather blasted face:

'Someones pinched me bike... I'm miles from home', said his plantiff voice.

The Cat stared deeply into the poor old fellows eyes... and then... burst out laughing. With that, he closed the window.

Shamefully, this display of utter selfishness and typical feline behaviour by the Cat caused me to laugh uncontrollably too!

The poor old fellow waddled off, head stooped against the driving rain.

We passed him later in Corporation road, the Cat giving him his favoured 'Cheshire Cat' grin through the Panda's steamed up windscreen.

I still feel bad about that incident today...

In general, death is an awful thing to work with and particularly shocking when its one of your own colleagues. We'd just come off parade on Nights and were in the yard checking our Panda's and refuelling before setting off on patrol. Dave Smith a well known and respected CID Officer waved to us as he came downstairs from the Jacks office. He roared off down the ramp and into Chester Street – as usual off home.

Within a minute we had a shout to attend a serious road traffic accident outside Cammell Laird's the ship builders, on New Chester Road. Several of us acknowledged the call and sped off to the scene. On arrival, we saw a car smashed literally to pieces around a lamp post on a bend. The vehicle was unrecognisable. A motor cycle Traffic Bobby was there and an Accident Unit. Apparently no one was in the vehicle. We were all standing around wondering which direction the driver could have gone in when we saw something move:

'Shit there's someone still in there!'

The Traffic Bobbies pulled an unrecognisable man out from the car. He was in a terrible state blood everywhere and with severe fracture and compression injuries. As I looked at him his eyes opened and his mouth moved. Behind me I heard a Sergeant ask;

'What do you think?'

'Likely to prove this one – definitely' said a Traffic Bobby in return. At that moment the mans' eyes closed.

It is said that the sense of hearing is the last one to fade away when losing consciousness.

'That's Dave Smith's Car!'

We all looked, following the Traffic Bobbies gaze. It took effort but sure enough it was. That could only mean that he mangled body on the floor at our feet was Dave himself.

'Shit, Holy Shit!'

Dave had probably heard those fateful words: 'Likely to prove…' and he would have known with utter certainty what they foretold.

He was dead on arrival at hospital…

In December 1983, Master Ho-Sing honoured me by opening a new Mantis Kung-Fu school at the Gymnasium in Birkenhead Police Station. A number of my coleauges attended, as did some outside friends. It wasn't to last sadly as Ho-sing was now ill and needed frequent hospital care. We didn't realise though just how ill he in fact was.

As 1983 drew to a close, I began to get the opportunity to pressure test my system even more. I was particularly keen to try out more refined pressure point hits and soon learned which were practicable. The festive season and the imminence of the superstitiously feared year '1984' meant that the Bucks and Yobs of the Town were even more keen to have a go – given the prime excuse of the coming police state… according to Orwell that is…. Not that any of those bastards could read Orwell!

1984 was indeed to be a fateful year. The first surprise was a change in attitude from Columbo – a little change but a change nevertheless. In January he admitted to me that he was now an Open University student too. In his case, he was studying the Arts and Humanities as opposed to the Sciences. That small effort at rapport from him took a few more months to settle into a workable relationship and a lot longer before mutual respect was to develop, but it did and I'd say that we eventually became good working friends.

On the Queensbury Gardens patch, I now had a regular 'Oppo' working with me: Lennie Philips. Lennie had been a Cadet on our section and had worked hard to get posted back to us. He liked the Queensbury area because it offered such a wide range of possibilities. Apart from the usual yobs and decent community folk, we also had some good class professional thieves and Regional Crime Squad 'Target criminals'. I was Pandering more than walking these days, and had effectively inherited the Panda that covered the Queensbury patch. My accumulated local knowledge and intelligence on criminals was deemed too valuable to lose by a posting elsewhere. I took Lennie under my wing and 'groomed' him as a potential successor – although I knew that he was probably along for the learning experience and that he'd likely end up in the Operational Support Division (OSD) – the 'Odd's and Sod's' as they were affectionately known. Lennie was even one of Master Ho-Sing's students at the Police Kung-Fu club.

A routine check on a motor vehicle near to Cleveland Gardens opened up a novel line of enquiry for Lennie. We searched the vehicle and found credit cards in various names, with receipts and statements all pointing to one address up in the North End. The driver of the car was arrested on suspicion of credit card fraud and interviewed back at Birkenhead. It transpired that he was part of a credit fraud ring involving a 'dead letter address' – managed by the local postman! The house number for the credit card accounts didn't exist. So, any mail going to it was intercepted by the 'Postie' and passed on to his cronies. They'd netted several thousand pounds in goods of various kinds. Indeed it turned out that there was more than one dead-letter address, and, that drugs were being imported posted to the same addresses. By the time the whole thing unravelled, it had become quite a major enquiry, involving not only the Police but also H.M. Customs and the Post-Office Special Investigations Branch.

Lennie and I worked well together, uncovering a lot of good class local crime; catching 'Fences' – receivers and dealers of stolen property – the essential 'middlemen' in criminal trade, and breaking up car 'Ringing' networks – which involved the stealing of vehicles either to order, or the creation of new identities for stolen vehicles to be sold on, or exported; drugs dealers – indeed the whole range of urban organised crime. All that on top of the usual: 'Trouble at Mill!' calls to the local pubs and clubs.

One of the quietest clubs in the Town centre however was 'Wirral Boxers'. Seldom any trouble at all – everyone was well behaved. Most of the time…

This evening though it kicked off quite early around 10.00pm. It was a hell of a fight, lots of 'ex-boxers' getting stuck in, and a lot of local yobs too. The doormen were overwhelmed and it spilled out into Argyle Street stopping the traffic and terrifying passers by. There was a general state of alarm at the Nick, boxing was something that they collectively understood, unlike martial arts. I remember thinking what a good thing it was that the bouncers at Rupert's or 'Sir James' clubs didn't go on a rampage. Now then they'd have had something to worry about. But, boxing is bad (or good) enough and this was an unpleasant situation. The section 'scrambled' in time for me to arrive and to end up getting punched for my trouble. I didn't have time to reason with him, so he had to go. I let him jab at me, but remembering that fight long-ago in Mersey Park, I didn't dance with him or attempt to box with him. I struck out at his biceps and shoulders with Mantis single knuckle punches and then turned a strike inwards against his carotid artery – a short shocking hit. Stunned his legs buckled and I eased him down to the floor and into a recovery position. He could wait there until things cooled down. The rest of the section were scrapping away and hauling bodies off into the van to go en route to the Bridewell. My man was put safely in, dazed but unharmed, so I decided to follow the retreating yobs around into Conway Street making sure they dispersed without causing any more trouble.

They ran up past the Birkenhead Market, and along Claughton Road. They were shouting and kicking out at peoples front doors. Passers by crossed the road to avoid them. It was obvious that this lot still had life in them and that they could start on someone innocent if not herded away homewards. Finally I stopped them in Oliver Street behind the Grange Road shops. Arguably, that was my first mistake, they c*ould* have just been allowed to disperse. My second mistake was getting out of the car and confronting their ringleader:

'OK you've had your little play, time to get off home'.

'Fuckin 1984 eh lads, listen to the pig snortin' away'.

'Yeah, yeah had yer little joke, home time now'.

'No. No pig, I ain't goin Fuckin anywhere; come on make me!'

At that point I accepted that this was going to be a fight and that I was outnumbered and isolated. Oliver Street lay between a vast car-park area and the backs of the Grange Road shopping centre. It was difficult to be seen in the shadows from the well-lit Claughton Road. This fellow had obviously sussed all that out and was going to go for it.

Just at that moment, a police van emerged from the junction with Grange Road itself and accelerated towards us. I was 'high' on adrenalin now and decided that I was going to address that fellow about his manners. I walked up behind him and having noted that he was right handed, I placed my right hand on his left shoulder, encouraging him to turn to face me with his weaker side leading. I didn't use my left hand as I wanted to avoid it being knocked across my mid-line and thereby perhaps isolating my own favoured right-hand side. He stopped, turned around, snarled and went to punch me with his now 'isolated' right fist. That was the justification for my next action. As he turned his centre line opened up and I planted a twisting–stirring front snap kick into his groin (the Playtex kick – to lift and separate don't yer know). Winded , he dropped to the floor. His mates were stunned as if such a move by a uniformed Policeman was totally unexpected.

Hmmm…well, they thought they lived in a Police state…
The Yob was locked up and charged with Assault on the Police.

In March, Arthur Scargill's National Union of Mineworkers

went on strike, and fell immediately into dispute with other coalminers who wanted to carry on working. This group formed the Union of Democratic Mine workers. Once again, as in Toxteth before, the Police became a political pawn. Margaret Thatcher was determined that her government would not go the way of Ted Heath's following the 1972 Coal Strike – into defeat. Massive amounts of police personnel were to be mobilised to travel around the country to sensitive areas and ensure that those miners who wanted to work, could work.

The overtime was a huge incentive, plus the fact that nobody believed that it could be as bad as Toxteth. Some of the younger Bobbies who hadn't been in the riots, such as Lennie, relished the idea of a bit of 'bovver' with the Miners. For myself, I resented the political aspect, even though I supported the right of men to go to work. It wasn't that simple however, and the government obviously had its own agenda. Consequently, I decided to stay on the Town and do my overtime there rather than get involved in political policing in far away areas whose local issues were totally unknown to me. There was also Pauline. She was my number one priority and she saw little enough of me as it was, without my disappearing from home altogether for a week at a time.

Those of us who stayed on the Town had to do overtime too however. There were fewer of us than normal so twelve hour shifts were introduced. Still it wasn't busy all the time, so I got some Open University studying in whilst I could. At that time, I met up with a Bobby from another section whom I'd remotely known for some years: John Forrest. John happened to see my psychology books and remarked on how he knew this 'professor' of psychology from Liverpool University. Would I like an introduction? Of course!

Graham Ball was an unlikely looking professor – but I put that down to my ignorance. After all I was an unlikely sod of a Bobby if ever there was one. He was unkempt and slack, both in appearance and manner. It seemed that he worked as a psychotherapist too, treating policemen's families for a whole range of problems. His 'contacts' ranged throughout the Force, from various uniformed officers to the Special Branch.

His 'school' of psychotherapy wasn't one that I favoured, but heck, he was a useful contact. Over a period of time he gained my confidence and we became friends…

Lennie was back after his first sojourn with the Miners. It had aged him a bit and although there had been trouble, it wasn't anything quite as bad as Toxteth. Still there seemed to be no end in sight so we all battened down for a long haul of twelve-hour shifts. We were working 7 till 7 nights, and I was on the Town Centre Panda again. Lennie was tired after his excursions, so that was reasonable excuse to double-up with him for the shift.

My usual Panda was off the road so I was allocated a pool-car. It had a new engine and a warning on the key fob not to exceed 30 mph until after a given distance.

Shit! That meant we couldn't raz round anywhere! Couldn't they give us cars with the bloody engines ready for use!

Soon after the shift had started we received an emergency call to attend at the junction of Prenton Hall Road and Woodchurch Road – a man going crazy with an axe!

Well, no time to lose on that one, so off we went chasing the revs as usual. The job was about 4 miles away, so even at a 60mph average speed it could be four minutes getting there. With an axe you could do an awful lot of damage in that time:

'Sod it Lennie, let's give it some welly!'
I enthused, quite ignoring the speed restriction on the Panda's new engine. When we arrived, the scene was deserted. No axe man… With no time left even to catch our breath another report

came through:

'GM32 from Control, report of a large scale disturbance at Wirral Boxers Club, Argyle Street'.

So, off we flew to that, the Panda's engine singing its nuts off happily as we tore down Borough Road at 80 plus mph.
On arrival, people everywhere, but, no fight. Other patrols who had been nearer had arrived first and calmed it all down.

And then? yep… *'GM32 from Control, the mad axe man is back in Prenton Hall Road again'.*

So….we tore off down Borough Road at 80mph plus etc etc. Once again, no one in sight and once again… *'GM32 from Control, the Wirral Boxers has kicked off, officer requires assistance. Any other patrols please for a scramble call to the Wirral Boxers Club in Argyle Street?'*

Before the message had finished we were tear arsing back in the direction of the Town Centre – flat out. You never ease up on an assistance call for a colleague.

By the time we were half way down Borough Road the Panda car began to lose power. Going through the red traffic lights at Whetstone Lane black smoke started to pour out from the engine compartment – by the time we arrived at the Wirral Boxers Club the engine was on fire and we couldn't see a Fuckin thing!

Meanwhile a hell of a fight was in progress: *'Holy Shite, Mary Mother of that fella from Bethlehem!'*

Lennie grabbed the fire extinguisher and I ploughed into the fight. By now I was as stoked up as the Panda's engine. One of our lads was flat out with a bust nose. Getting mixed up in it all, I noticed that I was somehow integrating the Mantis with the Hop-Gar system and that they were both being guided by the 'battle computer'. It felt just right and it worked efficiently and cleanly.

Afterwards, I realised that it had now at last become a part of me, and that the 'principles' behind the system, and its battle computer, simply selected the appropriate techniques and let rip. Maybe I'd had a hint about those two styles blending together in a complementary way?

There was a reckoning over the Panda car however. It was to be yet another 'make up some story your mother would believe' kind of thing about how we hadn't exceeded the running-in speed limit etc. Columbo received the report before forwarding it on. I fully expected that he'd 'bounce it' and that the shit would fly. But no, he endorsed it saying that we had come under extraordinary pressure and that I had to drive in the manner that I did in order to fulfil my duty.

Hmmm… very decent fellow indeed after all!

The 'Queensie' area demanded a bit of respectful give and take in order to oil the cogs of day to day life. Sometimes this meant passing responsibility over to criminals to do 'the decent thing'. This is for some Bobbies a laughable idea, but not for me. It all depends on the relationship that you have with your 'parishioners'.

As an simple example: One evening I was asked to execute an arrest warrant for a certain young man who lived in the Victoria Courts' maisonettes. I called at the house and found him there with his parents and young girlfriend. Normal procedure: 'lock him up' there and then. I knew his father, and I knew that he had tried his best with his family. I could also see that the lad himself and his girlfriend were very close. I have a heart, and it extends in a human way to what I can se of the 'bigger' picture:

'You know you'll go down for this don't you'.

'Yeah, I do'

The girlfriend was holding on close to him in tears…

'I trust your dad, and you're his son. Tomorrow, you get yourself down to the Nick and give yourself up – have a last night together with your girlfriend… I'll make sure that no-one else comes for you for at least another 24 hours…'

I went back to the Nick and to the amazement of the Station Sergeant told him what I'd done and that I was sure that the lad would come in and give himself up – without a fight, and that he wouldn't abscond.

That young lad turned up – voluntarily, and gave himself up for justice. He hasn't offended since. That's the kind of thing Bobbies should do more of in my opinion, get to know *people* – my old golden rule – let them get to know you too.

Birkenhead of course is full of characters, like the old prostitute: 'Scotch Betty'. Classic Betty, was a Magistrates Court appearance –one of many hundreds probably, when she was asked by the Bench about her home address – as she was in all likelihood of no fixed abode:

'Where is your home address?'

'Eh… I canny 'ear yer mister!'

'WHERE DO YOU COME FROM?'

'From mah Mothers crutch!' She answered truthfully of course… Such characters help to lighten up the staid ways of the law.

Then there was old One-Eyed-Jack the 'Puddle Collector'. Jack wasn't his real name, nor was he 'one-eyed'. It seems that his habit of standing on the corner of Duke Street & Corporation

Road masturbating away in public earned him his name. When exhaustion finally satiated his urgings, he would search earnestly for puddles of water to fill his black bin liners with. Apparently, the puddles restored his energy and allowed him to masturbate ever more vigorously. He was found dead face down in a Birkenhead dock, bin liner in hand. It seemed that he'd tried one puddle too big, even for him...

By now, it was apparent that Ho-Sing had cancer. I took him over to see John Cain and the two got on famously. John didn't bear out much hope however as the disease had apparently spread to the Liver. Under the pressure of his illness, Ho-Sing was baptised as a Christian and perhaps under pressure from his Christian friends he avoided returning to see John. Not that it would have made any long-term difference, but it was good for pain relief and he enjoyed travelling to see him.

I was still working with Pauline as Johns 'helper' and going up to Arrowe Park hospital for my psychotherapeutic work whenever I could. I was also studying psychology and training martial arts. It was to say the least a busy life!

The Wirral had always been something of an experimental area for the Police. It is a self-contained community, a peninsula naturally isolated on three sides by river estuaries and by Liverpool Bay. Accordingly, the Home Office decided that the Wirral would be one of the first areas to introduce the tape-recording of suspects, prior to its general application under the Police and Criminal Evidence Act (PACE).

This was a 'culture shock' to many officers, who had been used to more informal methods of interviewing and the taking of statements. Part of the general banter that made up 'Police Culture' was the practiced ability to lie under pressure. As a ritual, this was often seen at parade times prior to hitting the streets, and could form the basis for 'verballing'; the fitting-up of a suspect by literally putting words into their mouths and then reporting them under oath in court as the 'truth'. In practice, it must be said, verballing was actually quite rare and usually limited to nailing a known and active criminal who would otherwise have escaped justice. The parade room banter was a way of proving 'macho' style, your ability to face up to cross-examination by lawyers in the sterile environment of a court. Sometimes the mere threat of verballing was sufficient to get a confession. None of this morally justifies its use however, at least by everyday standards.

PACE put an end to all of that, and the Wirral Bobbies were amongst the first to feel both the novelty and the pressures of the new system. It slowed things down and allowed a number of guilty people to exploit the system and 'get off' with criminal convictions. No doubt a very small number of innocent people avoided being falsely convicted also.

One of the most frequent 'nuisance calls' that we'd get was to attend to 'Noisy Neighbours'. Sometimes this was due to celebrations at a party but more often it was caused by selfishness over loud music. Effectively, these were neighbour disputes and immediate police action focussed on preventing a breach of the peace. There was always the danger that if such situations went unresolved – then violence would ensue. So they couldn't be ignored.

This particular evening I was back and forth to one address in Tranmere. The road was very steep and poorly lit with access at the bottom blocked by concrete bollards. I was getting fed up of seeing this fellow and asking him politely to turn his music down: *'This is the fourth time I've called here tonight! Would you please turn that bloody music down!*

Expressionless, and in a monotone voice he replied: *'Your cars rolling down the hill'.*

'Yer Wha !?'

Maybe it was the way he said it.... Or maybe it was the reflection of a Panda car in his front window... silently passing the house downhill in the direction of the bollards...

'Shi .i . i . i . i . i. TTTT ! '

Ever tried running fast down hill when you're swearing? Lends a curious vibrato quality to the voice....

It was earlies, just on 'scoff change over', the cross-over time between the shifts two refreshment breaks:

'Any Golf Three patrol please, a report of an armed youth holding up a petrol filling station on New Chester Road – any patrols to respond please'.

Big Mal who was on the Rock ferry Panda, tore across the yard going for his car without a moments hesitation. At such times when one officer shows willing there usually follows a general charge.

A line of Panda's roared down Chester Street towards the New Chester Road. Mal was in front and me second. On arrival, sure enough, there were two youths on the filling station forecourt.

Mal was a brave lad and he didn't care too much for the dangers involved. I got out with him –separated by a distance – with the probable unconscious intention of presenting harder targets to the gun-man . None of that changed the fact that we weren't armed or couldn't have stopped him using the weapon if he had chosen to. In those day's Bobbies did the daftest things around the threat of firearms. No body armour or routine armed response units then. The rest of the Panda's blocked the entry and exit points to New Chester Road.

As I looked at one of the youths – the one answering the description of the one who had been 'firing' the gun – I saw to my amazement that he was a neighbour!

Big Mal was the first to speak:

'Mornin' sunshine, what's all this about shooting a pistol off at the petrol attendant!'

'Nah, not me mate, honest like.' said the youth.

I could see that Mal was sizing up the lad and thinking about how to get to him without getting shot. Courage was not something that he was short of.

'Mal', I said, *' I know that lad, he's a neighbour of mine'.*

I hoped that if he was a 'mad gunman' then my tried and trusted technique of "recognition" might work… Maybe he'd pull out a posy of flowers instead of a gun – it all being a mistake and then we could all go home.

'Wha' said the youth suddenly… *'Der yer mean this then?'*

Saying that, he pulled a black coloured pistol out from his inside coat pocket, pointed it skywards and fired!

Have you ever had that odd sensation, like you've run away, and yet somehow at the same time you're sanding still: feet feeling like they're glued to the floor in rock-solid shit?

None of us moved… in fact none of us said anything… Not even a token response like: *"Come on son let me have it!"* Fantasy policemen like Televisions' George Dixon, of 'Dixon of Dock Green' would have been most disappointed…

He fired the gun again, smiling to himself. I saw Mal lean forwards as if to rush him…

'It's a startin' pistol!' Laughed the youth.

'A Fuckin yer wah!' roared Big Mal.

'Put it down on the floor young man and come 'ere!'

The lad and his friend were arrested, and a statement taken from the petrol station attendant.

The youth was indeed a neighbour of mine, and I had the embarrassing job of bringing his parents down to the Nick in a Police vehicle. It is an unwritten rule that you avoid if possible anything to do with your own home turf – as in not shitting in your own nest. Not always possible as I was to find out on another occasion, but desirable nevertheless.

It turned out that this young lad was obsessed with the Army and accordingly it seems with guns also. He seemed to have no idea that what he was doing was potentially anything more serious than larking around with a toy cap-gun. The Juvenile liaison Office decided that he should be cautioned rather than charged with anything – and not long after, he did indeed sign up for Her Majesty's armed forces.

Looking back though, it was a typical Bobbies 'charge at the problem' only to find ourselves not potentially equipped to deal with it. Ah… the demands of duty…

Tear-arsing around in underpowered Panda cars had its down side too. I'd blown one Panda car's engine, and a second one followed – this time I managed to limp 'across the border' into the yard at Bebington Nick. I also had a brake failure at high speed, which wasn't exactly an enjoyable learning experience!

I'd had a hurry-up call to get to a disturbance at Queensbury Gardens. I was on GM32 but at another call in Rock Ferry. There was a certain Bobby on the GM 34 Panda. Since the Falklands War he'd acquired the nick-name 'Exocet' after the infamous anti-ship missile. This was because he always did his best to out-run you to a call– to be first there. Having got there however, it would be hands in pockets and two steps backwards, leaving others to sort things out. He wasn't a coward, or even lazy, far from it. He just enjoyed winding other Bobbies up…

So dangerous did the 'threat' become however, that the other drivers had to be more wary of the 'incoming Exocet' than any other hazard on the road! To get the point across we'd carry round rolled up balls of silver paper and flick them at him either on parade or out of the window of the Panda. This was after the 'aluminium foil' jettisoned by a target ship in the Falklands War to confuse the Exocet's radar guidance system – causing it to miss. It only served to encourage him and to take even more risks.

I drove down over Charing Cross and over the junction at Exmouth Street. It was a straight run through one more set of lights from here. Then, inevitably, I heard the screams of another Panda car engine chasing the revs to the redline and beyond. Exocet tore past – the waft from his vehicle causing my car to swerve violently. The next junction: Watson Street with Conway Street, had a hump in the road – good for 'four wheel take-offs' if you timed it just right and hit it at a fast enough speed.

The Exocet did a perfect four-wheel take off, with a deft landing some way on over the junction, I followed suit now quite caught up in the idea of beating him to the scene of the disturbance. My Panda 'landed' well enough but as I sharply decelerated and tried to apply the brakes – nothing!

'Shiiiiiii…T!'

The Panda hurtled over the next junction with Price Street, and on past a bemused Exocet who was now embroiled all on his own in the disturbance. I managed to turn the vehicle into Cleveland Street and stop it with the handbrake. Such experiences are humbling…. For a while at least…

Still, I learned a lot from ol' Exocet, and his local knowledge on the Town Centre was second to none…

One evening, I was back on foot around the Queensbury Gardens patch, when a report came in over the radio of an armed robbery at Charing Cross. Apparently, the takings from a local shop were being taken for deposit in the 'Night safe' of a bank, when armed thieves had snatched them and then made off at high speed – in the direction of the Gardens themselves.

I was in Price Street at the time, some distance away from Queensie. However, I did by chance glance into a nearby scrap metal yard. Lo' and behold there was a vehicle driving in that answered the description of that involved in the robbery. Sure enough, out from the vehicle came three men, again answering the general description of the robbers. I secreted myself behind the angle of a building – but allowing myself a good view. A Black Taxi – a Hackney Carriage drove into the yard, and the men transferred some bags and themselves into it. That was enough for me, I radioed the Control Room and requested the Jacks turnout to the scene immediately with some uniform back up. The response – '*we are too busy searching the area for the armed robbers!*' I asked again, and again, as available time for effective action dwindled away. Still nothing, it was as if there where too many chiefs too full of themselves for anyone to risk taking something like an actual sighting oft he robbers and their vehicle seriously!

It was decision time: do I go over on my own?

….NAH!

Get myself shot just to make a point… No chance!
By the time the our glorious 'defective constables' – er sorry 'detective' constables in the CID suddenly grasped what was happening it was all over…vehicles and robbers gone… Shows what can happen when 'local knowledge' in a Bobby isn't trusted or acknowledged. It also served to remind me that the

job wasn't worth getting myself shot for…

Professor Ball was making much of his Police contacts, and somewhat unethically for someone in his position proudly declared to me the nature of the 'problems' police officers and their families were consulting him for. They ranged from the usual anxiety or depression, through to sexual problems and bedwetting in children. I found his disclosures distasteful but by now I was inducted into a pattern of relating to him that seemed to make such things a 'norm'. I tried to get him to visit with John Cain as many other psychologists did, but he put it off saying variously that he didn't believe in any of that stuff, or that he was too busy. Oddly, none of the psychologist's who visited Cain seemed to have heard of him. One night after working at John's with a patient who had heart disease, I had one of the many strange experiences connected with Cain and his healing work. I was asleep at around midnight, when I awoke to see a whirling and circular tunnel suspended in the air above me. Within it was a TV screen like view of the man I had been working with. He was in pain and clutching his chest – I felt a terrible crushing pain too and started to call out. Pauline tried to rouse me but the experience was too intense. I saw the man, and his Wife – she naturally panicked and phoned for an ambulance. She then rang John and the man's pain subsided – and so did mine.

Next day I called at John's to find that the previous night at midnight in fact –just as I'd experienced it – the man had indeed had a heart attack, and his wife had called him. More than that she claimed that objects began floating around the house poltergeist like – as her husbands pain subsided.

A few days later, Eddie rang to say that Ho-Sing had died. Eddie had held his Master's hand, sharing his last moments – a true friend to him even unto death. Eddie was the 'first' of Ho-Sing's last generation of students…

On the day of the funeral, I was on Early shift and I was feeling a bit sleepy, and as sometimes happened I dozed off in the scoff break. I had what can only be described as a vision: an image of a tall golden cross- a Christian crucifix behind which was a golden octagonal pattern, like a representation, geometrically of a halo.

It seemed an odd thing to me, I couldn't be accused of being a Christian. Still, I was off that afternoon to Ho-Sing's funeral. Maybe my unconscious mind was just turning things over and the crucifix came up as something symbolic. It was a very emotional time after-all.

To my utter amazement, at the church: in which I had never been before, the coffin was placed before a tall golden crucifix, surrounded by a golden, octagonal, geometric representation of a halo… exactly in every detail as that which I had seen earlier in my 'vision…'

Despite being a Bobbies wife, Pauline had never quite gotten over the natural aversion the public have to being 'followed' by Police cars. It tends to bring out all sorts of paranoid behaviour, wide eyed starring at the speedometer or driving mirrors and a mind set tuned totally to the task of 'losing' the tail. All irrational of course, or perhaps something more primitive to do with avoiding 'predators'. Police cars patrol their beats like sharks and even being a Bobby myself I sometimes felt the primitive prey reaction when seeing a Police vehicle 'following' me, in my rear view mirror. In Pauline though this had developed into something of a compulsive art form. Picking me up at 11.00pm following afternoon duty was the worst. Maybe it was the darkness making it all the more subconsciously threatening… Anyway, one night I was delayed having arrested a couple of youths following a fight in Hamilton Square. I was going to be late off duty, so a couple of my colleagues in one of the Fast Response Cars decided to 'intercept' Pauline and tell her that I'd be late. They picked up Pauline's car in Borough Road, they tried flashing the headlights to cause her to stop… nothing, then they tried the blue lights – nice and gently just to give her a hint… after all it was her husbands shift that was on duty what did she have to fear?

Pauline's car took off down Borough Road with my startled colleagues in pursuit. Her driving became more and more erratic as she tried to 'lose' the High Speed Pursuit Vehicle. By now my colleagues were wondering what the hell was going on, maybe the car had been stolen! She drove down darkened side streets and alleyways, finally 'surrendering' next to some waste ground outside the Angel Inn in Beckwith Street. She was in quite a state, when my by now grinning colleagues delivered the message that I'd be late finishing work. Poor girl, even now years later she's still the same! The last 'chase' came long after I'd left the job and was in the car with her. This time it was broad daylight and we finished up facing an embankment at the end of a car park. The bemused Police Officer couldn't understand what was going on. Maybe she just likes being chased by men in uniform? She did have an apparent fondness for handcuffs when she was Sixteen… but that's another story!

Christmas day that year we were on Earlies, which meant getting up and in to work at an uncivilised and certainly un-seasonal hour.

So, Lennie and I decided to drive around the maisonettes' at 'Queensy' and wish all the yobs a Merry Christmas – through a loud hailer and in an appropriate local dialect… just so they'd appreciate us all the more don't yer know…

Final Police Years 1985 – 1987

"……..I've lost it, I can't carry on, I'm going home".

With Ho-Sing's passing, his students were leaderless. In my opinion, Eddie was the natural successor, as he had been the first of the last generation to be accepted by him, and, been there for him at the end. Ho-Sing's immediate family supported Tony Girven, who was skilled, and who had put a lot of time in. I carried on as before, with Eddie, and Philip Liu, one of the canniest fighters that I've ever known. I still saw Ken Liu and Master Chan, thereby keeping all of my martial arts options open. Ken was after all my first Chinese teacher, and his Hop-Gar style was still at that time my favourite Kung-Fu system. He also had a lot to teach, particularly about Chinese medicine, acupuncture and pressure point fighting. That combined with his Western scientific training in pharmacy was perhaps a unique combination.

Back at work, I was becoming very suspicious about Professor Ball. Something wasn't ringing true about him anymore. His knowledge of psychology had some very big gaps in it and he made some dreadful faux pas with respect to his psychotherapy theory too. So, I checked him out. Firstly with the British Psychological Society – the professional body for psychologists in the UK, and then Liverpool University itself. Neither had ever heard of him! Fearing the worst, I checked at MERCRO the Merseyside Criminal Records Office, and sure enough, he had criminal convictions going back to the 1950's, for burglary, fraud, deception, and theft. He was last 'employed' as an 'Education and Training Officer' in a local industrial firm, Lucas-Girlings Ltd of Bromborough. He was later (1981) convicted of stealing video film making equipment from the company – which he had used to make pornographic home movies; giving the video equipment to his 'patients' who where receiving help with their psychological or sexual problems. Ball then viewed the films at his 'pleasure'.

It seemed obvious that he was a potentially dangerous man and should be stopped. It was disappointing for me as I'd been taken in by him – at least up to a point. Sure he'd surrounded himself with Police contacts and friends, probably as a defensive smoke screen, but none of them had any academic psychological background and unlike me couldn't have been expected to see through him. What's more, Pauline had decided on a career change and had applied to Liverpool University to do a psychology degree. Ball had supplied a reference for her and it had even got past them, despite him putting himself down as a lecturer! Fortunately, she had also independently applied to do Occupational Therapy Training – without any involvement from him.

I needed someone to approach for advice about how best to proceed. I decided to speak to Columbo. His long CID experience was extremely useful. When he heard that Ball had taken in a lot of Police Officers and had a sting of convictions he agreed with me that something must be done to check out his activities. It was possible for example that he was involved in the sexual abuse of young girls, or to be in a position to gather sensitive information on Police Officers families – some of whom were in departments such as the Special Branch. If so, then that could be used – as was suggested about the Chinese towards me back in 1976 – to apply undue pressure, perhaps even to pervert the course of justice.

I approached the CID who weren't in the least bit interested. Even when I gave details of the numbers of officers (some of whom were in the CID) that had fallen under Ball's influence. A very senior ranking detective mocked the whole thing saying:

'It's not as if he's a Moor's Murderer now is it – just let it go!'

Columbo meanwhile put the matter before our Inspector: Dave Williams. He supported it outright and when I told him of the CID's attitude he calmly said that they would just have to be circumvented in the interests of justice. After consultation with the Inspector, Columbo took the information we had over to the magistrates court to get a warrant to search Ball's home. Instead of the regular CID, we seconded the Drug's squad – as it appeared from information received that Ball was illegally issuing diazepam (Vallium) a sedating drug, to his 'patients'.
It was then that I happened to bump into that senior ranked Detective, and told him what we were doing. He looked utterly shocked, sighed and said:

'It would be better if you didn't go ahead with this!'

I respectfully replied that I had to, and that my immediate supervision backed me up fully.

Apparently miffed, he stormed away. It's never a good thing to upset senior officers – they can have long memories. I was aware of thinking that I may have done myself a disservice in standing my ground, but, I felt that I had no option morally. I knew Ball was a fake and to have simply let it go would have allowed him further rein to do God knew what else in the future. I didn't like the idea of having the possible consequences of that on my conscience, nor did I think it a good thing that if it was subsequently found out that the Police had known all about him and yet chose to do nothing – maybe out of embarrassment – well… that would be unjustifiable.

The warrant was executed the following morning. Ball was used to me calling at his home, so he opened the door unsuspectingly. With me were a very good friend and Colleague: John Richey 'J-R' (of course!), Columbo, and the drugs squad. We confiscated numerous 'medical case notes' that he was keeping on various people including Police Officers, pornographic home video's, diazepam drugs, photographs, computer equipment and software, pornographic magazines and forged educational qualifications including a Doctorate Degree from the University of Liverpool, complete with the forged signature of the then incumbent professor of psychology: Dennis Bromley. He used that it seemed to win over his 'victims' confidence. Even his driving licence had the title 'Dr' before his name –falsely of course.

We then presented the CID with a whole list of specimen charges against Ball. We had even interviewed his family doctor about the issuing of the prescription diazepam drug. Nothing was to be overlooked. A very reluctant CID officer was allocated to the case. His taped interview seemed somewhat disinterested or even inept to me, as if he either didn't care or was out of his depth. It could have been either. Ball was bailed for further investigations. I carried on gathering evidence and taking statements in support of our proposed charges. I saw the senior ranked Detective again and joked:

'I suppose that this means that my posting to the CID is a non-starter?'

He gave me a withering look and said:

'You were told that to go ahead with this would be a bad move'.

'I'll take that as "no" then shall I Sir?'

The Miners strike was still in full swing, eleven months now and no end in sight. Locally we had yet another industrial dispute: this one at Cammell Lairds; and on nights that required Police attendance to make sure that the morning shift workers could get access past the pickets. This put a considerable extra strain on resources and so once again we were put on twelve hour shifts. One night, I was in for scoff and had passed over the Panda's keys' to a relief driver. I habitually left my radio on – we all did on Nights' as we had to be able to go out again at a moments notice to back one-another up.

As I sat there grubbing away, I heard a message from a Dog Section Officer who had attended to a violent domestic dispute above a nearby pub in Price Street.

Hmmm… nothing too unusual there, although its normally we who call up for the Police Dog's, rather than they ask for help from us.

As the radio messages passed, it became clear that there was a man in the building who had gone berserk and even kicked the Police Alsatian out of the pub. He was apparently punching through doors and plasterboard walls threatening to kill people. The Dog Man needed help, but, there were no patrols available, other than calling some in from Upton or Bebington! I got up immediately and started to sprint out across Hamilton Square towards Price Street. It was a clear, crisp night, but with that surreal quality to it that you get from a deserted street that's normally thronging with activity. From the radio it seemed that they had a name for this fellow, and that the licensee said that he did 'Kung-Fu'! Who the fuck was he? Darren Rowan…

Rowan was a senior student in the generation that followed me at Master Chan's. He was an aggressive and angry fellow – skilled and potentially dangerous. If he had indeed gone off like that and even booted out a police dog, well then that Dog Patrol Officer had better back off! I radioed the Control room and passed on what I knew about Rowan. I also offered to face him down personally – as we knew each other I reckoned that I might be able to talk him around.

Just as likely he would have a go actually – this chap was arrogant in the extreme and had the twin problem towards me of not liking me for leaving Master Chan's for Ho-Sing, and hating me for still being considered his 'Senior; in that school.

On arrival I briefed the Bobby about what I intended to do.

'OK, I'll just take the dog off and give 'im a wank, he needs calming down after that!'

I was aware of the peculiar nature of the situation as I went upstairs to where Rowan was. The run from the Nick had warmed me up, but I had to expect the serious possibility a fight with an enraged martial artist who had a grudge against me. Two issues were at stake here then: the law, and my status as a martial artist.

I knew that I'd seen too many Bruce Lee movies when my mind

spontaneously started to play the theme music from Enter The Dragon: as in the scene where Lee walks through the hall of mirrors! It took an effort of will not to creep around like him!

He greeted me like he had been expecting me:

'Hello Steve, long time no see!'

He seemed calm, but that might be deceptive…

'Hello Darren, likewise, long time no see'

'So, they've sent you to sort me out have they'.

'Who else would do?'

He reflected for a moment, and then:

'Yeah… OK. That's it then, I won't fight with you, it'sover…'

And over it was. Despite the feelings of hostility he normally had towards me, I believe that he had enough of a sense of honour to see that it all had to stop. I'd have gone blow by blow with him - man on man: and he knew that. But, I wonder, in the end, who really knows *why* he chose not to fight?

Later that Night week, we had a particularly cold night. Black ice had formed and the air was bitterly cold. It was my turn to stand with some of the other lads on the gate at Cammell Lairds. I'd driven the van down with the others and we'd all got out – all except one that is – who'd decided that he wasn't going to move *'for any fucking sod'*.

This fellow, Kevin Grey, was a relatively inexperienced probationer. That said he knew enough to do only what he needed to do, in order to get by. A quiet life option reduced stress considerably as a Bobby. He'd found his way around all the dossing spots on the Town – for grub, tea and booze, so that he would never normally need to get cold, hungry or thirsty at any time in any 24-hour cycle. He was a swarthy looking fellow with dark almost jet-black hair and a beard. For some reason he fancied that he looked like our blessed Lord: Jesus H. Christ himself. But we all thought that he resembled Peter Sutcliffe – the 'Yorkshire Ripper'. Anyway, all reason had failed to budge him and he was sleepily determined to stay put. This wasn't fair at all on the rest of us. So, Kevin would have to be helped to 'understand'.

The gate at Lairds was right outside a large roundabout at the end of the Rock Ferry By-pass. Its surface was like glass – just like an ice-rink in fact.

I decided to take Kevin 'for a ride' – seeing as walking didn't suit that is…

'Come on Kevin, either get out with the rest of us or I'll have to shake you up a bit!'

'Go ahead, do yer worst, I'll be dozing off'.

It was pointless trying to debate further. The van was a double wheel-based Ford Transit, laden with reinforced widows and armoured grills (after Toxteth). No limited slip differential, or anti-lock brakes, so – skidding would be the easy bit. We passed a bemused Sergeant who obviously wondered where we were going, and then suddenly it was like being back on the skidpan again. Kevin didn't drive – so he had no idea about how much control I had or didn't have over the vehicle. At first he hung on grimly but as the van spun and slid at higher and higher speeds he began to panic. The pickets however thought it a fine display– perhaps laid on especially for their amusement and entertainment and cheered us on!

But then:

'Argh.... owwww, eek.... help..... SHITING HELL!'

'What was that Kev, want me to go faster?'

'Nah....! STOP YER TWAT, STOP!!!!'

'Your word is my command!' I applied the brakes, hard, and executed an all-wheel skid at speed, off the roundabout and down the New Chester Road.

'Let me out...let me out!'

I let him out, as his hot sweaty breath clouded the freezing air. His blushed complexion made him resemble Lucifer more than our dear Lord. Funny, he always avoided me in a van after that...?

Back again on Earlies, I heard a call over the radio for Lennie to go to a flat in Birkenhead Park – a woman there was reportedly injured. Thinking that it was likely to be a domestic dispute – and that he may need back up, I called around to the address. The flat was on the top floor of a grandiose converted Victorian house, complete with its own driveway. There was glass all over the ground immediately below the flat and looking up above I could see a curtain fluttering away merrily from a broken window. Hmmm...no sign of blood or a body, so, no one has jumped anyway...

Going in and upstairs, the door to the flat was still open. What I saw almost surprised me...

A woman was lying back on a table by the broken window. She was attractive, young, with long flowing blond hair. She appeared to be wearing a red 'hippy style' dress – so far so good... Her expression was one of expectancy. Of what precisely wasn't clear. Lennie held each of her legs: one ankle in each hand, up in the air which exposed her naked lower half, as the dress had inexplicably blown back towards the window – and equally inexplicably she'd left her underwear off:

'Ah hem…!'

'Shit, Steve, I thought it was Columbo… give us a hand here!'

'Er what did you have in mind Lennie, I mean I can see that you've got both of your hands full at the moment'

'No, I'm serious, she's in trouble'.

Suddenly I thought that I understood:

'Oh, I see, she's in Labour! Bit on the slim side isn't she?'

'No yer dense git she tried to jump out of the window an' has badly cut her ankles. I'm holding them up to stop the bleeding, yer know gravity like…'

'Oh, well… what do you want me for then?'

'Me hands keep slipping on the blood and me arms are gettin' knackered!'

'Have you shouted up control for an ambulance?'

'No, how the fuck can I, me hands are full! I was hopin' one of yers would come round and get me out of this shit!'

'Lennie, I'm a married man, I shouldn't be looking at sights like that'.

'Are eh Steve, she doesn't mind, she was jumpin out the winder fer Christs's sake –what dus a little flash of fanny matter!'

Lennie was forgetting his manners:

'Please, language in front of the lady!'

'I don't mind who holds my legs'.

'Thank you miss, but I'll call the ambulance for now'.

I shouted up and passed the appropriate message. This was obviously a psychiatric referral, once casualty had done with her:

'One each Steve'.

'Eh?'

'One leg each, yer don't 'ave ter look...'

'Ok...Ok... just one leg'.

Hmmm...It was a nice enough flat, and the view through the broken window was picturesque: but, I mean, where else would *you* look?

When the ambulance arrived the crew came in as bemused as I had done: *'Ah hem... lady pregnant is she lads?....*

Kevin Grey liked his comforts.... particularly on Nights. The Miners strike was over at last and we were back to full strength on the Section. I was on foot on 'Queensie' alternating with spells in the GM 32 Panda. This night was very quiet; so Kevin, The Cat and I had met up in Argyle Street to pass the time in idle chat – and maybe get a brew somewhere. There was an all-night big snooker club in Town Centre –converted from an old cinema. Kevin liked snooker and reckoned that we'd be better off having a brew whilst appreciating his maestro-like skills on the snooker table. It seemed that he was well known there –

although it was mine and the Cats first visit.

After a while Kevin seemed to have an idea:

'Hey lads, they've got a Jacuzzi upstairs I believe: a fuckin huge one, as big as a small swimming pool. I fancy a splash myself, what der yer think?'

Hmmm.... Well, Cat's don't like water, and it seemed a bit risky to me but... we could always have a look I suppose.

'OK yeah we'll have a look see, and take it from there'.

Kevin seemed to know the way already. He was right it was an enormous Jacuzzi, more like a swimming pool really. In it however, were a naked man – whom I recognised as the boss of a local nightclub, and two girls, a curvaceous blond and a vastly buxom redhead – also naked. He was 'entertaining' himself with them without hindrance:

'Come in lads, they're yours if yer want em'.

Kevin was stripping off before he'd even finished his sentence. Looking around I saw video cameras up on the walls pointing towards the pool. A red indicator light showed that they were switched on. It was too late to stop Kevin, he'd jumped in wearing nothing but his truncheon.

Kevin was ostensibly a happily married man, but that didn't inhibit him here. The girls playfully 'accommodated' his truncheon: the knobbly hand-grip end of the shaft apparently being preferred.

The Cat was besides himself with amusement, but kept a wary eye on the cameras which panned around – presumably to focus on the action sequences being enacted in the Jacuzzi:

'Come on Cat. Discretion is the better part of valour here I think. Kevin must know the score – he's a bloody idiot though if you ask me, what with the cameras and all'.

'The women are well fit enough, I just don't relish getting in with Kevin and that fat Club owner – or you for that matter Steve!'

'Thanks! You didn't mind being intimate in Toxteth!'

'Yeah well, we were putting our truncheons to another use then!'

With that we left. Kevin didn't even notice….

Later that week, I was cruising around the Town Centre in Birkenhead, when I saw Pauline's Fathers car a white Mini 1275 GT: AMA 597K pull out of the Wirral Casino car park. He liked to gamble – and to drink and drive (also a gamble of course). He knew my Section was on nights yet he didn't seem to give a shit or think that he might be stopped.

I drew in behind him with the 'Police' roof sign illuminated and followed him as he crawled at around 20 mph all the way back to Jackson close. I Figured that he'd be sweating which is a small bit of revenge for all the problems that he had caused Pauline and I. I debated with myself about stopping him formally, and breathalysing (bagging) him – which would have been quite lawful. From his manner of driving, and from where I'd seen him emerge, I had good and reasonable grounds to suspect that he had been drinking an excess of alcohol. I let him sweat instead, all the way to his door.

Next day I blandly replied to an apparently innocent question from him; that I'd been on foot patrol for all of the previous night. I don't know if he believed me though. He was lucky, others would have 'bagged' him, and he'd have well deserved it.

Meanwhile, the CID seemed to me to be doing as little as possible on the 'professor' Ball investigation:

'This isn't going anywhere you know Steve' said the investigating Jack: *' I can't see anything worth chasing it up for...'*

'I can!' I interrupted... *'And I'm going ahead with it'.*

The Jack shook his head in frank disappointment. The senior Detective came over and gave his most revealing comment to date:

'This will cause huge embarrassment to the Merseyside Police if it gets to court'.

'I'm sorry sir, if you think that's a reason not to go ahead. My own supervision are backing it and like I've said before we don't yet have the full picture about what he's been up to. He should be stopped now before someone he "treats" as a patient ends up seriously hurt – if it hasn't happened already'.

He shook his head and walked off.

It's certainly possible that I was way off the mark in thinking that he simply wanted to avoid embarrassment to the police. It was equally possible for example that he thought it was unlikely to get as far as a court appearance, being thrown out by the Administration of Justice Department (Police Prosecutions) well before hand, and therefore a waste of time.

Still, I was determined and the investigation was going ahead....

The Cammell Laird's dispute took another turn, this time a Royal Navy destroyer had been occupied by pickets and we were told to go down and remove them.

Well, that was an interesting set of circumstances! If the vessel was still owned by the builders that was one thing. If, However, it had been handed over to the Navy then that was a much more serious situation. If then the pickets damaged it in any way, and in particular if any of them were daft enough to set fire to it… well… you could still be be-headed for 'Setting Fire to Her Majesties Ships'. The relevant law had been on the statute books since the Sixteenth century and had never been repealed. That would shock the buggers, getting themselves locked up to await execution on the chopping block!

We bussed down in the personnel carriers and approached the destroyer – a 'modified Type 42 class'. The White Ensign, the Royal Navy's flag fluttered from the stern.

So, looks like they have been naughty boys then!

Boarding the ship to 'remove' the pickets felt anachronistic – like at a latter day Boston 'Tea Party', and we should be wearing 18th century 'Red Coats' uniforms and carrying muskets and such like. In the end there was little resistance and a quick rout ensued with most of the strikers leaping off the ship and 'legging it' for the safety of the huge engineering sheds.

No crates of tea floated away along the dock, however.

The next night shift seemed quiet enough, up until mid week that is. Chris Llewelyn driving the Fast-Response car: GR31 had found the apparently dead body of a man in the North End of the Town. The corpse was in its thirties and lying face down on the pavement.

'J-R'and I were speeding off to a report of a violent domestic dispute – which to me seemed suspiciously coincidental, just a few streets away. I stopped the Panda by Chris, just to confer – the body did seem very dead indeed and it looked suspicious.

The body had fallen to rest on its knees. A stream of blood ran down the pavement from a small hole in the centre of its forehead:

'Looks like he's been hit straight between the eyes with a plasterers hammer or something similar' mused Chris.

Fleetingly, I wondered if he'd been shot…

All deaths are tragedies. Murders are very much so; all the more because of their suddenness and violence. There can be no dignity in such things.

Racing off to get to the domestic dispute we were met with a group of crying women standing in the street:

'What's happened love?'

'Oh, God… Oh God, its been terrible, terrible!'

'Try and calm down and give us the facts'.

'There's two fella's been fightin' over me, they started here and then they chased off towards Claughton Village'.

Hmmm…Call me slow, but that mans body was in that general direction…

'Can you give me the names and brief descriptions of the men involved please?'

'Yeah, names are John Moorecroft and Andrew Davies…'

The description of Davies fitted that of the mans body precisely. By now the CID had turned up at the scene of the suspicious death. J-R stayed with the woman getting a statement whilst I went around to see the Jacks. On Nights in those days you had token CID cover from the 'Night Jack'. This wasn't much more than that – a token presence, but if something 'interesting' happened, like a possible murder – then they crawled out from every pub and dossing hole in the Town. Jacks and pubs go together like the proverbial horse and cart. Obviously, its because they get so much criminal intelligence from their informants (snouts) in pubs, and has nothing at all to do with alcohol or any other kind of diversionary activity…

There was quite a crowd of them there when I arrived. Apparently, my name was as off-coloured as mud with some of my detective colleagues. It seemed that the Ball case had not endeared us to one another.

Talking to them, I attempted to get across the obvious connection between the violent running fight at the domestic dispute, just around the corner and the description of the victims' body. Nobody wanted to play. In fact nobody wanted to listen. I tried telling them that we had a name and an address for a suspect– still nothing – they were too busy they said to bother with an unrelated incident. They were the CID! J-R had taken a witness statement from the woman – who had been herself been assaulted, and wished to complain against Moorecroft. It seems that Moorecroft– a married man, was having an affair with this woman, at the same time that she was having another affair with Davies – who was also married. All in all a typical Birkenhead three-way domestic! However, it seemed that the two men had slugged it out and now one of them was dead.

Just to confirm the identity of the deceased, J-R went to the scene with the woman, whilst I set off in search of Moorecroft. The woman immediately made a positive identification of the body as that of Davies. Now at last, the CID started to take notice.

I called at Moorecrofts House. His wife answered and I asked if she'd seen him:

'No, he's off with his girlfriend, I've had it with him, I don't want to know – why what's happened?'

'Oh, nothing serious, I just need to speak to him about a small matter. If he comes home ring us and get him to call in at the station will you?'

She assured me that she would and I drove off. OK he might have been in there in the house, but my view was that he probably didn't know that he'd killed Davies and maybe he'd think that I was looking for him over the domestic. He'd most likely expect us to come down mob-handed if it was anything more serious, so the ruse could work. She should be able to trace him if as was more likely: he wasn't in her house, and then persuade him to call at the Nick.

I picked up J-R, by which time things had become even more complicated. It seemed, according to the first woman from the domestic dispute, that Moorecroft had *another* girlfriend! This one living in Oxton. The CID latched onto this and so off we went together in case our man was there. The woman occupier opened the door and the Jack, J-R and I went in. she didn't seem at all surprised to see us. Meanwhile the Jack missed the bleedin' obvious – yet again, so I asked the woman:

'Excuse me love, why is the washing machine going at four 0'clock in the morning?'

'I like to do it overnight, it's cheaper on the electricity – off peak you know'.

Meanwhile the Jack had found some pornographic magazines and was perusing them with interest.

I carried on with my questions…

'What specifically are you washing, is it John Moorecrofts

clothes'

'Yes'.

'Is it because they had reddish brown stains on them?'

'yes, like he'd been in a struggle yer know'

'And is that because they were blood stained?'

'Yes'.

'Leave her to me lads'... interrupted the Jack suddenly. Then: *'OK see yer...bye-bye Lads'.* It seemed that the Jack wanted us out of the way for some reason.

Puzzled, I went out to the Panda and made my pocket book notes up verbatim, including the conversations with the Jack and Moorecrofts girlfriend.

J-Rand I went back around to his Wife's house, and asked her again if he'd been home. No, she claimed; so, I asked her again to tell him to call to see me at the Police Station – in person that morning, as the matter was now a little more serious than before. She made her promise – and I decided simply to let it go at that and wait. Otherwise, the Jacks seemed to have everything under control... er... maybe.

At around 5.30 a.m. Moorecroft walked into the enquiry office at Birkenhead to see me – as requested. He probably had no idea Davies was dead at this point. So, I decided to get him into the Bridewell, behind a locked door before telling him. He'd already killed one man – it seemed, and he might just put up a fight or do'a runner'. I wanted the odds securely on our side.

He walked with me down to the cells and into the charge office. The Bridewell Sergeant Dave Jones started taking his particulars down on the charge sheet, 'booking him in'. Then suddenly he stopped, looked at me and disappeared. When he returned a plain clothes officer was with him:

'Who's this?' The plain clothes officer said.

'David Moorecroft'.

'Have you cautioned him?'

'Not yet, he's just given himself up to me in the front office'.

Then, turning to Moorecroft the Jack said:

*'I'm Detective Sergeant *****. David Moorecroft I'm arresting you for the murder of Andrew Davies....'*

And that was that – the arrest was snatched away from me and the CID apparently started the process of writing J-R and I out of the enquiry! Eventually, Moorecroft was to plead guilty to Manslaughterat the Liverpool Crown Court.

Afternoons' followed on from the Night shift. I'd just got a call to hurry up to an 'intruders-on' – meaning burglars – at a private house. I was blasting down North Road from Tranmere towards Prenton, when without warning, I felt the urgent need to stop the car and walk over into John Cain's. I hadn't seen John for a few weeks, so I had no real reason to stop just like that in the middle of an emergency call – it just seemed compelling…

Going in through the front door I heard myself say to John's Wife Audrey:

'Where's John'.

'In the Sanctuary'.

Trance like, I walked down the stairs into the annexe and

through the double doors into John Cain's healing Sanctuary.

The room was full, and John himself simply made a knowing eye contact. At that point, I fell out from my reverie and said a hasty goodbye, running back to the Panda and off to the intruders on call.

That night, I dreamt that someone married to one of Pauline's old friends from work had died. This fellow had been a patient of John's a year or so ago, but had given up. Since Pauline left work she hadn't had contact with the woman or her husband, and I had certainly not been thinking of them – far from it. Later the next day, Pauline received a telephone call from another ex-Civil Service colleague to say that her friend's husband had indeed died – the previous night. As in many cases before, the 'experience' in the dream was contemporaneous with the actual external event. He'd died as I was having the dream, timed precisely at 2.00 a.m. A coincidence certainly, but we'd been neglecting our work with John: and it isn't beyond the bounds of consideration that a 'psychic' event could serve to give us a gentle reminder of our responsibilities.

By now, including me, we had a total of five martial artists on the section. The others practiced a mix of Okinawan Karate, Korean Karate (Taekwondo), Shotokan style Japanese Karate and Western Boxing. I was still the only Kung-Fu man that I knew of anywhere in the force. It was good – sometimes, to discuss and exchange views with these people, but as in all walks of life closed mindedness and sometimes frank ignorance and bigotry arose. Usually this was the result of in-experience as this tends to produce the loudest and narrowest 'talk' of all.

One evening there was a disturbance in a Wine Bar in Grange Mount Birkenhead. There were doormen present, but perhaps wisely they resorted to calling the Police before going in themselves too heavy-handedly.

There had been some violence and drunkenness, but the main

problem involved youths refusing to leave. Two Bobbies had attended and thus far had failed to get them out. One big fellow in particular, who'd decided that he wasn't budging under any circumstances, blocked the doorway. Apparently, he was a rugby player and squatted low as if for a scrum and stood rooted. He was cursing and swearing that if anyone touched him they'd be flattened. One of my martial arts colleagues had tried gentle persuasion, but that had failed. I was the Town Centre Panda man, and decided to lend some assistance. Having ascertained that all the talking was over, it only remained to get him out.

His obligingly static posture allowed some assessment to be made of the problem, a little like a tree surgeon deciding where to prune away an unwanted branch. I thought an attack on his balance would suffice –not a single shot but light initial contact and then two rapid applications of pressure in a push- pull movement against his knee and ankle joints. Rugby players (like Tug-Of-War people) are great at rooting themselves firmly and resisting direct pressure. Few it seems are experienced at responding to the rapid application of oppositely acting unbalancing forces against their leg joints. Anyway, this fellow certainly wasn't…

Much to his surprise, he fell sideways out of the door:

'Eh…yer Fuckin…ARGH…!'

I was then 'downhill' to him on the slope of the road that made up Grange Mount, and he decided to use his rugby skills to his advantage in rushing at me for a waist level tackle. I managed to get my arms and hands up in the air and clear of his grasp. Then, leaning forward and moving backwards, to 'run-out' some of the momentum in his attack. Finally I stopped and braced myself into a long forward stance with a single bent leg leading, and simultaneously planted two single knuckle 'pressing-punches' into the carotid arteries on either side of his neck. Abruptly, he gurgled, and fell forwards – I had just enough balance available to catch him as he fell face downwards towards the pavement:

'What happened there?' asked a bemused Taekwondo Bobby. *'Oh, he had a sudden loss of blood pressure I suppose – must be because he'd put his head down too low when he ran at me: happens to drunks sometimes'.* He didn't believe me, but then it wasn't 'in his system' to use techniques like that and this fellow was blind to anything that wasn't 'correct Taekwondo technique'. A case of 'seeing is disbelieving' you might say. A case of being 'in denial' more like it! To be perfectly fair, it wasn't the art of Taekwondo that was at fault, it was him. He just happened to be a fully paid-up and practicing representative of it.

The next day was 'quick-change' from Afternoon's to Earlies' i.e. finish at 11.00pm and back on again eight hours later for another shift. Around mid-morning I got a call to go to Queensbury Gardens, a report of a burglary, with the suspect identified as one of the Hughes's – one of the two involved in the fighting some years back with the Vietnamese Boat family.

The informant was new to the area but he knew the suspects name:

'It was Deggsy – yer know Derek Hughes'.

'Sure?'

'Yeah I saw 'im, he was in me bedroom goin' through me things, he ran off out the front door like, an me money's all gone like – 'bout fifty quid!'

'Will you give us a statement'.

'Definitely!' This was duly taken. By the time I called round for Deggsy, his family were adamant that he wasn't there; in fact he was in the Magistrates Court that morning, so he wouldn't be doing over people's flats on his way to court now would he?

Well, pardon me for even thinking it!

A quick check revealed that he was in fact up before the bench that morning for allegedly stealing a car. So, I decided to arrest him at court – an unorthodox procedure – but it appealed to me to think of snatching him from under his defence briefs (Solicitor) nose!

The Police have a somewhat ritualised relationship to the Magistrates Court –beyond the rituals of the Law itself. The magistrates get to know officers pretty well from frequent court attendances and in return Bobbies and lawyers get to know one another too. It becomes something of a game as solicitors go through theatrical manoeuvres to impress both their 'client' and the bench. Solicitors themselves regard the magistrates court as 'the Police Courts' and don't rate working there as something particularly lucrative financially. Some briefs however are notorious for defending any old sod, including the case of one late Tory MP – who was also a solicitor, defending a burglar who was separately charged with committing burglary at his own home! I'm still left wondering what comes first with such people, is it the right of the accused to be defended, or is it simply a living for a brief? No prizes for guessing which explanation is favoured by many Lawyers!

What I had in mind was going to create a stir. Still the old place needed a bit of a shake up. The previous year I'd been in court and was 'directed' by the magistrates to evict a man who was drunk and clearly disorderly in the courtroom itself. I did, and outside he became even more disorderly, so I arrested him for 'D & D' – simple? Er…no. He pleaded not guilty and inexplicably was acquitted by the same magistrates who had 'directed' me to evict him in the first place! Their Worships Olympian powers of reasoning must have seen something that I'd missed–whatever, it was beyond me! Deggsy had a permanent grin on his face, and it was particularly polished when he saw me come into the waiting area for the court.

Maybe, he thought he knew something that I didn't? His solicitor grinned inanely at me – we'd met before, and would again no doubt. I smiled my best 'Cheshire Cat smile in return':

'Derek Hughes, Court Number One' called an Usher.

I let him get in through the doors, and then in sight and hearing of the bench I stopped him, placed my hand on his shoulder and said:

'Derek Hughes, I'm arresting you on suspicion of burglary at Queensbury Gardens this morning… You are not obliged to say anything unless you wish to do so, but if you do, anything that you say will be taken down in writing and may be given in evidence'

'Awww Shit Man…! Why yer layin that trip on me?'

Jaws dropped, eyebrows lifted, solicitors were lost for words (well that's a first!).

He 'coughed the job' on tape back at the Nick, and was charged and bailed – to appear at Birkenhead Magistrates Court….

Pauline didn't like the loneliness when I was working Afternoon's or Night's. Her family didn't help her and probably hoped that the isolation would put an unbearable strain on our marriage. Of course, it wouldn't, but I came home and checked that she was OK as often as I could. One evening, I telephoned to find her very upset. Apparently a gang of around a dozen youths had been terrorising her and physically threatening her at home, whilst I was away on duty.

That was red rag to a bull time. I grabbed the nearest Bobby – who happened to be on overtime from another shift – Gordon Wilson, and took off in my Panda at full pelt:

'Where are we going?', asked Gordon – no doubt thinking that I'd had a hurry-up call –actually I was on my scoff break.

'Home: my Wife's getting threatened by a gang of Yobs. I want you there to make sure that I don't kill anyone!'

'No problem Steve, I'm with you on this, we've got to look after our own families: after all who else will!'

His sentiment needed no confirmation…

I got a description from Pauline and then set off on a search. The area were we lived had had a sharp increase in its teenage population – a direct result of the 'Babies Boom' in the 1960's. these lads weren't babies though – they were drugged-up louts who knew that I was away at work and thought that they'd have some 'sport' threatening my Wife. I stopped a few locals and narrowed the search down to one name in particular. Driving around – I found him. I wound the window down and asked if he was ******:

'Yeah, so wha!'

He went to walk away… I grabbed his jacket so hard through the window that his head yanked forwards, I pulled again and he smashed his nose on the roof of the car. I released my grip as he fell back…opened the car door and then side kicked him straight into a conifer tree hedge. As he bounced out I grabbed his neck and pulled him forward onto an elbow strike – and he fell down....

An elderly male passer by chanced a remark:

'Just like when we were kids that – they need a good cuffing they do terrorising us old folks! Now, when I was a lad.....'
Groan!

Back in the Panda:

'Well, I didn't kill 'im… lucky for him'.

'Christ, I didn't know you could do moves like that!'

'Yeah well, it's amazing what you can do when your loved one's are threatened!'

Pauline was never bothered again.

The year drew to a close with a quite unexpected shock: John Cain had died suddenly after a heart attack. His immediate disciples concluded that he had overworked himself – he'd had a heart attack before, but he'd kept on working seeing between 70 and 120 patients a day for 'hands-on' treatment. He smoked heavily and drank whisky like water. He was a thoroughly good man – who'd dedicated his life to the health of others. He sincerely believed in what he did, and of all the supposed psychics that I've met he was the only completely convincing one.

He was very good to Pauline and I. Before our wedding, Pauline's Father threw her out of the house because she had refused to give me up. John kindly provided us both with a bed at his home. He had been prepared if necessary to stand-in for Joe and to give Pauline away at our wedding. He also generously paid for our wedding cars. His kind are sadly rare – and I shall never forget him. His son, 'Young John Cain' continued on for his Father, afterwards.

1986 brought another early and sad loss, Big Mal had left the Section and gone over to the Wirral Police Control Room. He'd been taken ill and died tragically young in his early thirties from a pulmonary embolism (blood clot on the lung). He had a Police funeral: the best attended that I've ever seen, in Bromborough Church. He was married with Children, and sadly missed by family, friends and colleagues.

By the time Ball went to the Crown Court in Liverpool, the

charges against him had been reduced to a token handful – not amounting to anything that serious. No further investigations were carried out by the CID. He pleaded guilty to forgery and was sentenced to 9 months imprisonment; six of which were suspended. Nevertheless, the case attracted attention from the local press. Our prosecuting Council was Mr Brian Leverson QC, who was better known for his IRA trials. That had been secured by Columbo – through his contacts. Leverson embarrassed the CID and the Police solicitors by suggesting to them that I had a Lawyers brain and should train to be a Criminal Law Barrister – it was a nice sentiment…

The trial and circumstances of the case made the local papers and indeed there was some embarrassment for the Police. In the Crown Court itself the defence lawyer and the Judge pointed out the naivety of the Police in getting involved with such a man as Ball. That criticism included me of course. I had been taken in too, but, I wasn't going to let any personal embarrassment get in the way of him being brought to book. I felt vindicated, but wondered if there would be any repercussions to follow from my senior colleagues.

Inspector Williams short-listed me for a Police Advanced Driving Course, which I looked forward to with mixed feelings. It was a great opportunity, but the pressure was going to be extreme. The Standard Car Course for Panda's had been tough enough – but this was going to be an order of magnitude greater in terms of the demands that it would make.

Essentially, you were expected to drive with the utmost polish and skill at extremely high speeds on public roads. In my case I reached 130 mph (as measured on a calibrated speedometer) on a dual carriageway coming into the Speke area of Liverpool from Runcorn Bridge. This was an 'unmarked' Police vehicle with no blue lights or sirens. The margin of error at those speeds is less than hair thin.

We were trained in high-speed pursuit techniques – and had to practice chasing instructors in other cars – even around a skidpan. On the skidpan We had to miss 'obstacles' representing other vehicles and pedestrians, whilst weaving around after the instructors car. We were timed on the skidpan and had to be within a few seconds of the chase vehicle in order to pass the assessment. We had a theory examination as last time – the pass mark being much higher at 86% for a 'Class One'. Same on the two final assessment drives: one a normal 'advanced drive' the other a 50 minute high-speed pursuit. In the pursuit assessment an instructor would role-play a bank-robber driving a getaway vehicle and he would do his utmost to lose you. In my case I 'picked up the Bandit Car' on Chester City Ring-Road and then shot off after it all over North Wales, returning to finish just outside Chester Zoo.

You were constantly marked – negatively, as in starting off with 100% and then having points deducted for the slightest mistake. You could pass at Class One or Two and qualify as an Advanced Pursuit Driver or return with a Standard Class Three – only for Panda's.

I did my best and achieved Class One.

Coming back to the section after such a course is a recognised hazard. You are so hyped up at first that the fall in adrenalin back to a 'normal' level often means that accidents happen. Indeed we were warned that the first month back after the Pursuit course is the most statistically dangerous time for Police traffic accidents. The problem is that you are so relived at getting through, and so thoroughly trained, that errors paradoxically occur more easily. Despite my previous Panda experience I was to make a very basic error almost immediately. We had just rolled in to finish our shift from earlies at 3.00pm when a scramble call came through from the Fast-Response car covering the shift changeover period.

I looked around and saw that no one was in the least interested in responding. The morning crew had psychologically 'booked off' and the afternoon section had not even engaged themselves yet. I felt a sense of outrage similar to that at Upton years before when the Gofer had offered 'printed invitations' to the section to turn out to a pub fight at the Woodchurch Hotel. I grabbed a radio and retrieved my Panda car keys from the Station sergeant and informed control that I was turning out. Still full of righteous indignation, I ran to the Panda, started her up and then reversed straight into a 12ft high steel pillar!

I was 'grounded' immediately, and investigated by a Traffic Department Sergeant. This fellow was a motorcycle officer. He liked to wear his cap with its peak 'slashed' – slanted down over his eyes. That, and his wearing motorcycle uniform 'Jodhpurs' gave him a Nazi like appearance – which was in fact fully justified by his manner. He was livid at me and ranted that non-traffic officers should never be given Advanced Pursuit training, and if he had his way I'd never drive a Police vehicle again. He was well over the top in his attitude, and well off-mark with respect to the implied relative merits of Panda Drivers to Traffic Officers. Panda car drivers as I've mentioned before drive under much greater pressure and have to do so in less well powered and equipped cars. Still, he wouldn't have wanted to have heard that, so I thought it wiser to let him have his little rant. He did write a damming report however, but my Section Inspector overruled it. Nevertheless, I was lucky. Technically, it wasn't a Road Traffic Accident (RTA) as it hadn't occurred on a public road –but in the Station car park. If it had been on a road, then I'd have been certainly prosecuted for careless driving and had my Police driving authority revoked. That incident served to 'pop' any inflation that may have arisen in me due to my achieving a Class One.

On getting my Police Driving Authority restored, I was put straight onto "Golf Romeo Three One" (GR31) one of the two fast response cars on the section.

Back on Nights again, there was a hell of a wind getting up. I was parked up with my temporary 'Oppo' Lennie inside Birkehead Park:

'Shit Lennie, that wind's strong, we'd better get out here before a tree fall's on us!'

'Golf Romeo Three One from control'... interrupted the radio.

'Go ahead over'

*'Report of a large tree down in ***** Road, a man believed to be trapped in his car'.*

'Roger en-route'.

'Bloody Hell, no sooner had I said that and one's down!'

We sped the short distance to ***** Road and sure enough just on a bend about halfway up, an enormous tree had dropped down spanning the width of the road itself and crashing through the garden opposite. It had a huge trunk, and underneath it was a Volvo 240 saloon car. The roof, of course was flat, the edge of the trunk had just caught the drivers' head, pressing behind his neck and trapping it against the steering wheel. He was conscious and able to move his eyes. His breathing laboured. I called Control for an ambulance and the fire service, and then I remembered that a doctor, a general practitioner, lived about 30 metres away.

Leaving Lennie with the injured man, I ran the short distance to the doctor's house and knocked on the door. It was 4.30 a.m. and she didn't seem too happy to be woken up:
'Doctor, a tree has fallen across the road about 30 metres away. It's trapped a man inside his car. He's injured and needs medical attention'.

She looked at me like I was an alien, or perhaps educationally sub-normal:

'You know first aid don't you?'

'What?'

'You know first aid surely, what do you want me to do?'

'You're a doctor!'

'Yes, so!'

'I'm asking you, officially, to attend an injured man, he could die!'

'Wait and get an ambulance!'

And with that she closed the door…

I couldn't believe it. I knocked again and asked her again and once again she refused. I told her that I would submit a report to the effect that she had been asked to attend the scene and had refused. Her response…? She slammed the door…

Getting back, Lennie was still trying to verbally console the injured man. The fire Service and Ambulance arrived at the same time – and proceeded to argue about how to cut the man free. His neck was braced, but it had been broken.

He died of respiratory failure later that day.

Disgusted over the doctors behaviour, I submitted my report – but nothing came of it. If the poor man had been driving only one or two miles an hour faster or even slower the tree would have missed him. He'd only travelled about 40 metres before the accident. The doctor, his neighbour, had been his G.P. OK she may not have been able to do anything, but no –one knew that at the time, and a few kind and reassuring words may have eased his suffering.

On Afternoon's I received a scramble call to a Bobby being assaulted by a deranged man at the scene of a domestic dispute. On arrival, the front door was wide open with the sounds of a violent struggle blaring out. The house was a 'Coronation Street' style terrace. Going straight in from the road into the living room; I could see furniture smashed up and signs of blood splattered over the walls. Then, I saw my colleague wresting frantically with a man who was holding a large marble ornament. Blood was gushing forth from the top of the Bobbies head.

No time to lose! I went straight for the hand holding the weapon. His grip was strong and I couldn't break it by forcing his fingers apart. His arm was stiff with rage and very resistant to attempt sat locking. I'd have to break his concentration and get his attention away from his hand. It was all made somewhat the worse by my unfortunate colleague who was held by the man in a powerful grip – making the three of us fall about Elephant-like all over the tiny living room. I resorted to a pressure point hit to stop this man: the so-called 'breath blocking point' on the exposed ribs at the side of the chest. With his arm being held upright, it was an appropriate choice. He gasped and dropped the heavy object onto the floor. His grip on my colleague also broke and at last we had him subdued… I thought…

There was still some more fight left in him though… going out of the front door, he twisted away from my colleagues grasp and hit me in the groin with a toe-ended kick shouting:

'There! That'll part yer piss flaps!'

Well, his anatomy was well out… I mean, *"piss flaps!"*

It was tempting to welly him back: but, he was to all intents and purposes beaten . I had *never* been one to hit prisoners gratuitously. – It was a kind of 'parting shot' that he launched at me – and my colleague was injured & bleeding. So, our prisoner needed getting back to the Bridewell as soon as possible – into safe custody – and my colleague needed medical attention.

It taught me a lesson though… about parting shots…

Bobbies are used to dealing with gruesome incidents, but, one kind of 'job' above all others at Birkenhead was if at all possible avoided. This was dealing with a dead body in the River Mersey, or one floating in one of the docks.

The Mersey is a lot cleaner now than in those days, but that didn't stop the annual event known as the 'Police River Swim' which involved a group of Merseyside officers jumping off the back of a Ferry Boat and swimming a couple of miles down stream. It shows the power of 'tradition' in such things that even with the inevitable infection and gut wrenching sickness that followed for many of the participants, it was still highly popular.

That popularity did nothing though for anyone's enthusiasm for handling a decomposed and sodden river corpse - usually coming complete with various aquatic life forms attached to it. One Sunday of earlies Hannibal was informed by a member of the public that something looking like a body had been seen floating in a dock near Duke Street Bridge:

'Shit, Shit, Shit…!'

Hannibal decided that an effort should be made to 'lose' the body, or, better still, 'encourage it' to float out on the tide, hopefully over to the Liverpool city side of the river. Hannibal was last seen hovering around the dock with a long pole purloined from one of the ships.

A body later turned up over the Mersey in Bootle docks….

The Bridewell had its own unique sub-culture. It was a kind of soft-posting if you could stand acting as a jailer and feeding prisoners grotty food with plastic knives and forks. I never relished the idea of being responsible for the prisoners safety, after all sometimes there are accidents or suicides, and deaths in Police custody tend to attract shit like nothing else.

Some Bobbies had in been there for years, growing old and morose with their saturnine jailer's duties. Some of the younger Bobbies too, who went in. started to take on a premature fossilisation of their personality – maybe it was the confined spaces?

There was one older Bobby in particular, an Irishman: Patrick McLaughlin who although decent enough in other ways, was one of those who liked to punch at you or even kick at your groin. Maybe it's a 'dominance' thing, like you get in a Baboon troupe. Maybe he had a red arse to go with his red hair?

Anyway, this morning I was in with a prisoner, and was too preoccupied to play his little game. He'd been in the Bridewell for years and it was part of his routine to kick out at you. I saw the leg and foot move and then…

I kicked him on the ankle, then with the same leg 'flick-kicked' his balls and stepped through on top of his back foot taking his balance. His head had come forward as he doubled up in pain and surprise- so to stop an incoming (accidental?) head butt, I hit both his shoulders with a springing double palm heal hit which threw his body back against the wall. Almost choking in

Teaching at the Instonians Rugby Club: 'Mantis Kung-Fu' 1986

Group photo 'Ho-Sing Kwoon Southern Praying Mantis Kung-Fu' 1986
Standing on left of picture: the authors brother Wayne Richards (Karate & Kung-Fu) Seated from left to right: Dad (Tom Richards – Boxing) Author Steve Richards, Si-Fu Kenneth Liu Hop-Gar kung-Fu, Si-Fu Philip Liu Praying Mantis Kung-Fu Peter Collins Praying Mantis Kung-Fu, Si-Fu Eddie Berry Praying Mantis Kung-Fu

pained surprise he slunk down to the floor:

'Morning Pat, nice to see you on good form!'

The other Bridewell Bobbies starred in amazement, and I got on with my work. Pat Mclaughlin never bothered me again.

I was training harder than ever for my Kung-Fu. In fact I'd noticed an emerging change in attitude within myself. I was becoming much more aggressive towards my martial arts friends and contacts, and this was becoming a risk for me at work. I'd always been wary of 'losing it' but I was beginning to care less and less about that. It wouldn't matter to me anymore if I seriously planted another Bobby even. I was aware of this new mind-set and I tried resisting it, but pressures were building up on me at work and they had it seemed to come-out someway. These work pressures were to prove decisive for me with respect to my Police career, and the aggressive attitude now developing within me had its secret purpose too, but I was unaware of this consciously at the time. For a while at least the tension was ducted into training but also into something a little more shameful.

I was drilling myself for explosive speed and would daily practice 'countdown punching' of 1,000 punches per set for up to six sets at a time. These would be performed at sprint speed whilst wearing wrist weights. The effect was a tremendous burst of fire – designed to overwhelm an adversaries ability to cope. The targets for these strikes would be pressure points and the impact surface a single-knuckle. The idea was to emphasise a Mantis kung-Fu technique and then to hone it to perfection. Similar drills were executed for other techniques all combined with a gruelling fitness regimen.

I lost a lot of weight but I became *very* fast indeed.

Away from work, I'd given up the psychology degree and work

at the hospital. John Cain had died so I had a lot of free time to train. I was refining my combat model still further and trained my mind and brain to function literally like a battle computer. That kind of 'computation speed' enhanced my increased physical speed, making close quarter range my favoured fighting distance. I trained hard on punch bags and speedballs, but reduced weight training to a single exercise – the bench press. This is the simplest and the best resistance exercise for building up a near perfect punching platform. It develops all the upper body muscles you use in hitting without over-development of antagonistic muscle groups. I worked hard for endurance and explosive power and not muscle bulk.

Master Chan asked me at this point to go back to his school and to take-up where I had left off as his Senior Non-Chinese student. This clearly bothered some of his newer people who saw their status under threat. They also commented on how much weight that I'd lost. To which I coldly and simply emphasised how I was so-much the faster and fitter for it – if they would like to try me out….?

I *didn't* want to go back to Hung-Gar – for me now the Mantis was *the* style to do. Curiously, Master Chan very graciously ignored my by now unfettered arrogance – other than to say: *'You thought that you were clever going to Ho-Sing eh? Well, you don't know that much do you! If you like Mantis Kung-Fu, you should have gone to another Master, he's here in Liverpool, he is the Grandmaster of that style – the Son of Ho-Sing's Master – but you don't even know who he is hah, hah!'*

Hmmm…I thought I could hear the sound of an over-inflated balloon popping…

I was training with Eddie Berry and still learning as much as I could from the Liu's. Eddie had introduced me to Ho-Sing's nephew: James Ho, himself very accomplished in the Mantis style. From him I was able to get even more of the classical style and then to refine it further by processing it through my 'system' and its battle-computer. I asked him about this 'other Master', but his Chinese inscrutability and fogging batted off all of my questions. James had a great way of telling you things – once you already knew them! It was like one long guessing game, as soon as you found out something, you were told it 'officially' but with a few teasers added on. A bit like with a Playstation task where you have to find clues and solve riddles to get to the next level.

James Ho, I now know, was 'cultivating' me to take this style of Mantis out into the public arena. It had long been a secret art, taught only to Chinese of 'Hakka' descent. Recently (mid 1970's) it had been taught to non-Hakka Chinese and some Westerners, but none of its then current generation of younger practitioners seemed to have the drive to make it well known. James Ho literally 'managed' me, and my development in that style, and 'assisted' me to go through the proving-ground tests that were to follow.

It was at this time that I perhaps quite shamefully got involved in challenge fights with other martial artists, both from the Mantis system and other schools. 'Comparisons' as they are called, are common enough – but tend to fall short of the excesses that I now indulged in. I would travel to meet with instructors and do my best to beat and humiliate them in front of their students – I rationalised this by saying that many of them were arrogant and that they taught crap, having no real fighting experience – just talk and dreams. Some of my Mantis colleagues (for example James Ho and Eddie Berry) encouraged it, as I was being successful and thereby enhancing the styles reputation. I didn't care much who I went up against – whatever the grade rank or status of the teacher, Chinese or English. I became quite obsessed with 'pressure-testing' against anyone and if that meant physically flattening them well then so be it. Once that 'battle computer' switched on, it ran me like a machine – 'they' had to go down or I'd die in the attempt.
I went to one fellow whom I known for a long time: an English

instructor of the Hung-Gar style under Master Can. I showed him up so badly that three quarters of his students walked out on him there and then and came over to my newly opened Mantis school. Those that stayed with the Hung-Gar instructor had the most to lose by leaving – they where the senior students who had status under him. It couldn't have been for any other reason (I thought) as they had been 'planted' just as he had. It didn't seem to occur to me that they may have found what I had done distasteful. In other perhaps less moral ways, it was justified: those that came with me and subsequently have stayed with me ever since, have flourished and achieved much more than those who did not.

This was a relatively mild incident compared to some others, but it affected my conscience later on quite badly. The instructor lost so much face and credibility that he turned to drink and became a down and out alcoholic. If I'd left him alone then maybe he'd have got by. He was harmless enough, except it could be argued that his teachings were misleading people. He teaches Yang style Tai-Chi now.

I taught as the Liu's had done to me thirteen years earlier – hard and fast. Now though, It was a different 'Mantis' that I was doing: one with a scientific, pressure testing edge to it, augmenting its classical foundation.

All went well so to speak until during a free fight practice with a muscular seventeen stone friend; Peter Collins, I punched him on his flexed elbow bone and broke my hand. I kept on sparring with him for another thirty minutes ignoring the pain. Not the best of ideas. Pete later became a British & European Super-Heavy Weight Thai-Boxing Champion. I was off work for six weeks… OK, so I couldn't punch any sod any more, but, there was a lot of other things to do hitting wise and so I kept up the work-load.

When I got back to Police-work though something else had

changed. All the supervisory officers that I had known had gone. Columbo, Inspector Williams… all transferred. In their place were some unknowns: a new Inspector and two sergeants…

J-R and I were down to do some riot-shield training at RAF Burton Wood in Lancashire – then an active U.S. Air Force base. The authorities there let us use some of the huge aircraft hangers to set up mock riot situations. By now – late 1986, there were a lot of Bobbies in the job who'd missed out on Toxteth, and they needed some realistic training. The 'trainers' though had to have credibility, and in the Police, as in the armed services, credibility was often associated with rank and 'sweet F.A.' else.

You may remember that I mentioned one of the 'few' male Bobbies on the section back in 1981, who didn't go over to Toxteth? Well, one of them was now a 'Public Order Training Sergeant' – a man who'd managed to avoid most confrontations right through his service – he had in fact, in the words of Kid Curry:

'Never seen an angry man in his whole life'.

This true paragon of the warrior breed, was now presuming to teach *us* how to work in a riot! It was too much to bear, and he sensed my complete scepticism and lack of respect. As power-merchants will when threatened – he puffed himself up with all of his rank and authority:

'I'm the Sergeant here and you'll do things how I say, that's an order!'

Well, one of the 'exercises' was going into a room, supposedly a flat, having entered the building as we did on the Woodchurch, in order to arrest a suspect who would 'resist' us forcibly. This Sergeant had his ideas about how it was to be done –which to J-R and I was totally unreal and asking to get yourself hurt. J-R had been an Operational Support Division (OSD) Bobby in the riots and fought hard hand-hand in the streets. I'd say actually that of all the Bobbies that I've ever worked with, he was the one that I'd most rather have with me in a scrap. We'd worked well together now for about two years, and faced many a threatening situation. He was also a martial artist – Karate, Boxing and latterly some Kung-Fu with Eddie. So I knew that he was utterly reliable.

The 'suspect' was padded up and prepared to give some stick. The first lads who went in were easily overwhelmed when trying to follow our blessed Sergeants instructions. Funny isn't it how often 'instructors' of all persuasions set their students up by teaching them things which then fail immediately under any real pressure. It has a demoralising effect and yet paradoxically increases the status of the instructor. A neat trick that...

When our turn came however it was going to be different…

First off, we split up into two – which foxed our man straight away – the exercise supposedly involved the two shield men staying together. Then, we wellied the suspect with the shields – edge first – and boxed him into a corner by pressing the shields full length against him. Backing off –which 'bounced' him out of the corner; I dropped my shield and laid into him with rapid-fire martial arts blows onto his padded up shoulders and hips.

Thus drilled – he spun out of control and fell back at which point, J-R gained the mount position, kneeling on the 'suspects' shoulders and applied an arm bar across his throat. A strangulated gurgle indicated his submission:

'Q.E.D.!' I shouted, to cheers from the other Bobbies.

'What are you doing? That's not how I said to do it!'

'That's how it's done in the REAL world!' I replied.

'That's insubordination!'

'That's the Fuckin truth!'

We weren't allowed to play after that… Hmmm….

Back at work, I found that the new supervision, whom I'd known for less than a full working week, had completed a 'Staff Appraisal' on me which was supposed to take into account my previous two years work. Obviously, they couldn't have known me well enough, but, they completed the forms nevertheless and sent them with a covering report up to the Divisional Superintendent. I knew nothing of this until coming on for Night's I was summonsed to see the Superintendent. She showed me the report, which in my view was not only unfair but was a complete travesty and a fabrication. You are meant to sign your staff appraisal forms to say that you 'agree' with the comments. If you don't which is very rare, the matter has to go before an Assistant Chief Constable. I refused to sign, pointing out that these people had only known me a few days and yet their comments were detailed and in my estimation frankly false. I requested that Inspector Williams, who had been my Section commander for 6 years be asked to complete an appraisal on the basis of how he had known me to be.

A week later Mr Williams arrived in person. To my surprise, he was now a 'Chief Inspector' and coincidentally posted to the Complaints and Discipline Department (responsible also for internal complaints and investigations). He spoke to my new Inspector and Sergeants in private and then came over to me:

'Steve, the appraisal completed by your new supervision in no way reflects you as I have known you to be for the past six years. I have written my own appraisal of you which if you agree with it you can sign'.

Chief Inspector Williams appraisal report was accurate and fair, so I signed it without hesitation. I did find all of this a very troubling development however. I had long heard 'whispers' that some senior officers were displeased with me for pursuing the Ball case. Maybe it was a 'spin-off' from this new 'attitude of mind' that had been creeping in to me, but, it seemed in my view that what had been done to me with respect to the appraisal was a little too orchestrated to be coincidental.

If, by sticking with the Ball enquiry I had made enemies: then it was reasonable to *fear* that something might be done to discredit me at some point too removed in time to be easily connected with it. *If* that was the case, then the recent appraisal could be an opening shot.

I certainly *believed* that was true. I had no evidence, but then how else could I explain why it had been done? Policemen had been 'fitted-up' before by colleagues. I'd seen it done in various forms many times. I even began to wonder if the next thing would be an 'illegal substance' or perhaps stolen property being planted in my locker…

Meanwhile, I had to 'get on' with those very supervisory officers who'd now been humiliated by a Complaints and Discipline Department Chief Inspector. In feeling vindicated however, I was like the cat with the cream. I wouldn't speak at all now to the Inspector or the Sergeants not even to acknowledge that they so much as existed. I just cut-them-dead. That's a very difficult thing to do in everyday police work. The closest I'd come to speaking to them was talking about them in their presence, directly in front of my colleagues – about how they had tried to fit me up on the staff appraisal. They *never* challenged me once: which to me showed that not only were they wrong, but that they *knew* that they were wrong. All of this made for a very difficult atmosphere, and I began to sincerely believe that if I set even one foot wrong then I'd be set up properly next time…

One night I was driving GR31 around the precinct checking property, when I chanced across my Okinawan Karate colleague and one of the Korean Taekwondo Karate men. It was a still and quiet night and we got talking amongst other things about the chances of getting yourself 'beat up' in the line of duty. They had a lot less service in than me, and hadn't had anything like as many fights behind them. They were martial arts types though, so, in many sad respects there was a lot of 'armchair bravado' coming out – especially from the Taekwondo guy. The Karate fellow was younger, a tougher lad really who suited the ethos of his martial system. He had guts but the other one was suspect far as I was concerned. Anyway, I said that the Okinawan Karate lad had better resign himself to the inevitable, it *was* going to happen sooner or later. Then, I returned to the car and drove off back up to the other end of the Town, on a call.

Within minutes, the front window of 'Burton's' in Grange Road had been smashed –within sight of my two colleagues. Three men had gone in and were ransacking it. The young Karate Bobby went straight in after them, thinking that his Taekwondo Oppo was close behind… He wasn't, he was nowhere to be seen. The Karate lad put up a fight – as I'd have expected of him, but he was knocked down as the men made their escape. The Taekwondo Bobby? He'd gone around the back of the premises, into Oliver street – quite a distance away to call for assistance and to make sure that the thieves didn't come out of the back!

Well, I'd say that was an error of judgement – to leave a colleague to go in on his own like that… Some might say that the Karate Bobby made the mistake of going in alone? Maybe. But the other fellow didn't show that he could be trusted in a *real* fight in my estimation: some would have called him a coward. It proves that it isn't the 'martial art in the man, it's the man in the martial art' that counts.

Birkenhead had a high level of car crime, and in recent weeks one place in particular: Hind Street, was being heavily hit. Hind Street was behind a Merseyrail underground station and led to the old Birkenhead Gas Works. It formed a makeshift 'spill over' car park for people shopping in Birkenhead Shopping precinct. I was on Afternoon's, and I asked Pauline not to park our car there – a red Ford Fiesta Sports, because of the danger of it being nicked. It was a place that she habitually parked in, but, she assured me that she wouldn't…

At around 6.00 p.m. I got a call to go to Hind Street, report of a car being stolen. I roared off in the Fast Response car thinking" God, I hope Pauline didn't Park there!" On arrival, there was nothing to be seen not even an informant. Anyway, I couldn't see our Ford and thought that Pauline had done the sensible thing.

Then…

'Golf Romeo Three One from control'.

'Go ahead over'

'Please return to the General Enquiry Office at Birkenhead Central – person waiting to see you…'

Hmmm… who can that be?

It was Pauline! I'd been sent to my own car being stolen!
I was upset, mainly because she'd ignored me. She was upset partly out of embarrassment and partly because all of her revision notes for her Occupational Therapy exams were in the car!

The next thing didn't help one bit:

'Serves you right for buying a Ford Take-Away' …. It was one

of the Sergeants'!

I had my radio in my hand – a heavy-ish object, enough to fracture someone's skull.

Enraged, I lunged at him with it. J-R grabbed me saying: *'Don't Steve, they're trying to goad you… it's how they want you to react'*.

The Sergeant stood impassively, in my belief confirming with his eyes what J-R had said.

'OK'. I said – feigning calmness. Inside I was boiling. How much longer before I do snap, or, before they 'fit me up' with something? It wasn't an irrational fear… Bobbies have fitted one-another up before. I was certainly being goaded, and this fellow had been humiliated by the Chief Inspector. As for the rest… well, real or imagined it was the kind of stress that I was under now, constantly. Gradually it was becoming almost too much to bear.

Our car it turned out was used in a robbery at a jewellers shop some 12 miles away in Neston. The proprietor had thoughtfully thrown a brick through the windscreen of the car causing it to crash and the thieves to abandon it. I took Pauline by Police vehicle out to recover our damaged car from Neston Police Station: which was just 'over the border' in the Cheshire County Police area. They seemed amused, but it wasn't funny at all to us. The ignition had been 'barrelled' and was now only operable with a screwdriver. Fortunately, all of Pauline's notes were still in there –untouched.

Later that week, by now brooding over what I believed in my own mind lay ahead for me; I attended at a superficially simple domestic dispute. The woman who owned the house wanted her boyfriend to leave following a series of more violent domestics that had passed between them in recent weeks. I was tired and preoccupied, so my concentration was lower than usual. I said to the man:

'Come on you've got to go – outside'.

'Outside?'

'Yeah, outside!

It didn't twig with me that this was taken by him as a direct challenge to fight with him.

He went into the kitchen, which would normally have alerted me that something was wrong, but as I said, I was preoccupied and my attention was lowered.

He walked past me to the front door and I followed him out to make sure that he left safely.

Suddenly, he turned and started wildly swinging at me with a huge kitchen knife! I caught his next swipe by passing inside his arm – allowing the knife to slap harmlessly on the back of my heavy Police clothing. Then, I knocked him to the ground and affected an arrest.

I hadn't been alert enough to realise that when I said *"outside"* he'd taken that as a challenge, nor had his visit to the kitchen been a clue either. I reckoned in retrospect that my reaction to his attack – to get inside his swing by going forward was about right. If I'd have retreated that would have encouraged *him* to go forward even more intently – and I would have lost the initiative. Not ideal perhaps, but in this instance, forwards was better than backwards.

Some weeks later, I got a note from the Prosecutions department to say that he'd been *"bailed to a higher court"* – a Police euphemism for him being dead. Apparently, whilst awaiting trial he'd taken his own life. That gave me cause to reflect, as people who harm themselves in that ultimate way are sometimes equally capable of doing it to others.

That Christmas was a time of uncertainty for me… What would 1987 bring?

My martial arts school was going well at least. It was housed in the 'Old Instonian's Rugby Club in Prenton. We had full use of the Club's facilities including the field for running and even sparring. We had our own mats, punch bags, air-sheilds, focus mits, speedballs etc. and, traditional Chinese flags.

I felt more in control of my circumstances at the school, which was factual of course. I was however becoming concerned psychologically about the effects of recent stress in my life. I was under threat – attack even by my supervisory colleagues. I believed that I had a number of enemies in senior ranks within the force – specifically in the CID. These were people that I couldn't fight and win… If I did nothing I lose. If I act in self defence… I lose…

The strain of apparently not knowing from which direction I'd be attacked next began to drain me. I knew I'd lost it when I went with J-R to pass a death message to an elderly woman whose son had committed suicide by jumping from the top of a block of flats. I went in feeling very 'dissociated' almost like it wasn't me, I said:

'You know your son lived in a block of flats?'

'Yes, is he alright, what's happened officer?,

'Well, he jum…. At that point, in mid-sentence, J-R pushed me out of the door and away into the street.

I didn't react, it was like I couldn't. When J-R came out of the old ladies house some considerable time later I said:

'John, I've lost it, I can't carry on, I'm going home'.

'Best thing Steve…'

My reaction and lack of feeling had disturbed me. I've kept a copy of the telex message about the suicide to this day.
I knew enough to realise that I was being detached – defensively by my own psyche– shut down if you like. If I wasn't at work, then maybe I'd be safe from "them". My G.P. signed me off with depression – which is a reasonable diagnosis – medically speaking. If you feel that you are helpless and cornered eventually anyone will be 'shut down' or switched off.

My being signed off ill, seemed to cause some ructions back at the Nick. The supervison became all friendly towards me – no doubt I thought because if I was asked why I'd gone sick – then I was likely to say because of them and the pressure that I was under. I was off for a couple of months when the Inspector and a Sergeant called around to my home virtually begging me to come back to work.

Hmmm…missed their sport that much eh!

This happened on and off until I was offered another community beat – this time with my own parade station (Well Lane) in Rock Ferry, Birkenhead. There would be no direct supervision and I could arrange my own hours as I wished, with no Night duties. That would have been a dream posting for some. So I accepted. No sooner had I done so however, than I was sent to the forces Chief Medical Officer for a medical examination. He let me know in no uncertain terms that if I didn't hack it on my new duties, then I'd be retired on medical grounds – without argument.

Well, I went to Well Lane, but despite the control I had over my work, it wasn't the same. It wasn't Queensbury Gardens or even Upton. Anyway, I was a class One driver and my skills were being wasted. My heart wasn't in it, and the depression came back.

One morning, in full uniform, I had to stop myself, quite literally stop myself physically, from walking under a bus on the Old Chester Road…

In a daze, I went back to Well Lane Nick, put my radio on the desk and went home.

My G.P. signed me off and I was called to see the Chief Medical Officer once again at Hatton Garden. It was a formality of course. I was pensioned on ill health grounds on the 10th August 1987.

When I took my warrant card and uniform in on the last day itself, an old Bobby said:

'Anything you want to say to the Chief Superintendent before you go – it's your right'.

'No, he won't want to listen to anything that I'd have to say to him'.

This was the Chief Superintendent who'd walked in on our Section's parade some years back and said:

'Stress! Anyone here thinks that they are suffering from stress can fuck off and empty bins' for a living!'

What would be the point?

I decided not to have a 'leaving do'. It was all over for me and the Police. That, I later learned was a mistake. I should have had a 'leaving ritual' to mark the end of a career that had spanned my life from age 17 to 30 – my 'youth' effectively… As a result for some years afterwards, I was to have recurring nightmares that I hadn't left the job, I was still 'in it' or was being called back, immediately and without prior notice. In effect it took several years to actually 'leave' the Police service psychologically.

My own medical notes contain a letter from the force Medical Officer to my then G.P. It seems that as far as the Police were concerned, I had developed what would be today called a 'post-traumatic stress disorder' (PTSD) following my head injury in Toxteth. The 'flashback' character of the nightmares and vivid dreams would certainly support that view. Also, the gap in years' between the original trauma, and the manifestation of symptoms. One of the riots many: perhaps latent, Police victims.

Maybe…

Certain triggers within the Police service had to be pulled in my belief, for any latent effects to become manifest, and there had been plenty of those. Still, it's only fair to consider that the PTSD diagnosis could have been accurate, and indeed that it may have been behind some of my perceptions of my supervisory officers in the final months of my service.

However, my psychological training up to that point and certainly my psychotherapeutic work that was to follow, suggested something more akin to an early mid-life crisis. A need to completely re-evaluate myself and the direction of my life. The Police had given me a fantastic amount of real-life experience, but perhaps it had run its course for me, and I had to move on, or 'be' moved on, forcibly from within my own being. The martial arts were 'claiming' me, and a huge amount of tension polarised between them and my psychological studies. Over the following years, between that 'rock and a hard place', the next emergent stage of my personal development was to unfold…

I did one last thing: I called back to the Queensbury Gardens district and said my goodbyes to Canon Burns, Mrs Smith, and to Liz Maddocks, Billy Kinch and Eve at the Birkehead Boy's club. It had been fun, and I'd not let *them* down…

It looked like the stress in the Police had won. I'd lost my career, my livelihood and it seemed much of my 'status' as a man….

Afterlife

"Tell me of your childhood dreams"

I left the Police with no idea what the future would bring. Financially, it was very difficult, as Pauline was at college and we only had her student grant and a very modest pension from the Police to live on. The martial arts were going well, but I wasn't drawing any income from it. It seemed that after all those years in the Police I was back to square one. I hadn't finished my Open University degree, but I had completed a number of courses. Maybe if I went full time to university I could finish it off and develop a career in psychology? I was keen to get started immediately. Enquiries revealed that I'd be too late for that years intake at Liverpool University, but Liverpool Polytechnic was running a combined honours degree in: 'psychology with handicap and disability'.

Hmmm…might be interesting that, and it dovetailed with Pauline's training as an Occupational Therapist.

In those days (1987) British academia was divided between universities of the traditional kind that could award their own degrees through Royal Charter – and polytechnics – who had their degree's validated externally by the Council for National Academic Awards (CNAA). As in all systems, snobbery reigned and 'Poly's' were looked down upon as being second best to the 'red-brick' *real* universities like Liverpool, from which you could get a *real* degree. Entry standards for the universities were somewhat higher than for the polytechnics – so the snobs had some apparent 'evidence' for their critique.

I was acutely aware of the difference between the courses– status had been taken away from me by losing my job in the Police, and entering student life in a 'second best' capacity didn't help the feelings of shame at being 30 yrs old and without financial or even as yet academic standing.
Nevertheless, I entered into the spirit of things as fully as I could. But, some difficulties presented themselves almost immediately…

In our first year we were obliged to do some Social Science modules, one of the lecturers: Pamela Palmer, was decidedly anti-police and used her lectures as an opportunity to lay down her apparently 'Marxist' manifesto. OK fine, everyone can have an opinion, and academic opinions are there to be challenged – aren't they?

Well, she didn't know I was an ex-Police Officer, so I kept my own counsel. The crunch came however, when we were asked to do an essay on Police crime recording practices. I did so, using my insider knowledge gained over the previous thirteen years. The essay was trashed publicly by Palmer, who still had no idea of my background. I couldn't take any more and said:

'My essay is based on what really happens in the real world, not on your Marxist fantasy about it'.

'What! You've written rubbish, where's your proof for your opinions!'

'Simply thirteen years of recording crime day in and day out as a front line Police officer. Where do you get your evidence from

eh?'

Hugely embarrassed she lost it completely and changed the subject. Of course, she had now become yet another 'enemy' for me to contend with, and as in the past, it was someone who had a say in my future. The psychology aspect of the course was OK but nothing challenging. In fact it was too easy – I was getting top grades without even trying. Worse still, there was no attempt at seeing things more broadly. Psychology was abstracted out from the fuller human context – there was for example no appreciation of the biological sciences – or of medicine. The whole thing seemed ineptly constructed and indifferently presented.

There were many 'mature' students enrolled on that course. All apparently shared the one goal of becoming 'clinical psychologists'. Liverpool University ran the clinical courses and favoured their own graduates for the limited available places. I did some research and found that at that time *no* Liverpool Polytechnic psychology graduate had ever succeeded in getting onto a clinicians course. Yet, many of the psychology department staff at Liverpool Polytechnic, blithely allowed people to form the impression that such success was routine, and as such that they could easily go on and specialise as clinicians. I pointed all of this out, and got a reception equally as welcome as that afforded to Banquo's Ghost in Shakespeare's' Mac Beth.

Since those days, things have changed very much for the better. Liverpool Polytechnics now 'Liverpool John Moore's University', and many of its psychology graduates do indeed go on to train very successfully as clinicians.

Pauline was by now suggesting that I leave the psychology course, and transfer over to do Occupational Therapy. Occupational Therapy is a state registered profession and had the advantage of certain employment upon completion of its training. It also considers medical science within its remit, and has therefore a much broader aspect to it than psychology. So, I decided to give it a go and applied….

In January and February 1988, Brian McKinney my long-standing friend in the martial arts, invited the Liu's and myself to join with him and Master Jifu Huang (formerly of Singapore) to initiate a new 'British' Chin Woo (Ching-Wu) Athletic Association. Brian is a very 'low profile' martial artist, which belies his true status and skills. He is probably one of the most well rounded non-Chinese Kung-Fu men in the UK and has an impeccable background in Japanese martial arts too. He also has vast street and 'Door' experience which gives authority and credibility to his teachings. I respect him very much. In support of the new venture, the Singapore Chin Woo Athletic Association where invited over to the UK and performed a number of promotional and celebratory displays around the country.

One was held in Birkenhead, in the Grange Road West Sports Centre and it was here that I first met with the Wing-Chun Kung-Fu Master: Samuel Kwok. Master Kwok is less well known, at least publicly, as a Si-Fu of the Tibetan White Crane style as taught to him by his maternal uncle Luk-Chi-Fu of Hong-Kong. This system is a branch of the Tibetan Lion's Roar art and so was very closely related to my Hop-Gar.

We got on very well indeed, exchanging ideas and experiences. Eventually, we trained together and I started to study Wing-Chun formally under him. It was nice to have contact with this system again after so many years. Master Kwok performed the 'Bai Si' or 'Closed Door' ceremony with me, accepting me into the Wing-Chun family as his disciple in Kung-Fu. Master Kwok's skills are very high – in fact I believe him to be the very best of his generation within the Wing-Chun art. He is a natural successor to his Si-Fu's (Teacher's) Grandmaster's Yip-Chun, and Yip-Ching.

Group photo 1988: Master Samuel kwoks' Wing-Chun Kwoon in Blackpool Author standing far right. Second right: Bill Wilson – authors' senior student. Standing far left: Si-Fu Shaun Rawcliffe. Standing centre: Master Samuel Kwok

Author weapons sparring with Master Kwok: Wing-Chun Butterfly Swords versus Mantis Eyebrow Level Pole: Blackpool 1988

My Mantis school was flourishing as ever, and sadly, I was still indulging in challenge fights and public put-downs of other systems instructors. At this point however, something happened that was to signal the beginning of the end of such things for me: James Ho finally introduced me to the Mantis 'Grandmaster' that Master Chan had told me about some time before. This was Grandmaster Lee-Lien (Jimmy Lee) the son of Great-Grandmaster Lee-Yin-Sing, who had been Ho-Sing's teacher. In March 1988 he visited my school with Si-Fu Paul Lee (Lee-Po), who paid me the ultimate compliment in saying:

'You move just like Ho-Sing did!'

Grandmaster Lee allowed me to acknowledge him as 'Si-Bak', which means 'Senior Uncle teacher' i.e. someone of the same generation as your teacher but who is senior in rank. He taught me more of the Classical Mantis system, including various traditional weapons, empty hand techniques and practical applications.

The Lee-Yin-Sing branch of this Southern Chinese, Bamboo Forrest (Jook-Lum) Temple Praying Mantis Kung-Fu, is very different from the other systems that fall under the umbrella of Southern Mantis boxing. Lee-Yin-Sing himself (d. 1970 in Hong Kong) was a very colourful character. He had been a Kung-Fu brother of Wong-Yuk-Gong and Lam-Sang, who themselves went on to found separate lineages of the Jook-Lum Temple art. Wong claimed the true direct inheritance from their joint first teacher: Cheung-Yiu-Cheung. Lam-Sang however, later claimed to have left Cheung and studied directly with the monk Lee-Siem who had been Master Cheung's teacher. Meanwhile, Lee-Yin-Sing, who had set up his own school in the Hong-Kong New Territories, had 'disappeared' for six years, only to return and announce that he had accompanied another monk 'Lee-Tik'

back to the Kwangsi Temple (the original home of the Jook-Lum Mantis) and there learned a 'different' version of the Mantis art. Wong-Yuk-Gong had been a great friend of Lee-Yin-Sing, but it seems that he may have taken Lee-Yin-Sing's claims as an affront to his status. Some say that the two fell out acrimoniously and Wong allegedly wrote a letter to Lam-Sang (by now resident in the USA) denouncing Lee-Yin-Sing and his teachings. Lee-Yin-Sing wasn't to be stopped however. His school flourished, but he was a very hard teacher – beating his students up if they couldn't stand the force of his technique. Ho-Sing, his student, represented Hong-Kong as a Mantis boxer in Taiwan in 'Kong-Sau' (hard-hand or full contact) tournaments in the 1950's, placing as a semi-finalist in the heavyweight division.

Being taught by Grandmaster Lee under the watchful eye of Si-Fu James Ho

The version of Jook-Lum Temple Mantis taught by Lee-Yin-Sing, from the monk Lee-Tik was so different in terms of its technique, power generation and basic training that many refused to believe that it was in fact the same art. Ho-Fong, who was Ho-Sing's brother was studying with Wong-Yuk-Gong, but when he saw the skill of Lee-Yin-Sing's teachings he decided immediately to switch over and study under Master Lee.

As time passed, Lee-Yin-Sing acquired a formidable reputation as a challenge match fighter – a tradition carried on by his students. Lee-Yin-Sing travelled extensively around South East Asia, teaching in Hong-Kong, Malaysia, Singapore and even Vietnam. Today his system is known as 'Lee-Gar' (Lee Family) Mantis in Malaysia and Singapore, and '13 Roads Mantis' in Vietnam – named after the single long 'form' that he taught, with each section being a 'Road' that expresses the essence or 'laws' of the art of Mantis boxing.

Some trouble persisted between the descendants of Wong-Yuk-Gong and Lee-Yin-Sing, in the UK in the 1950's and '60's. That is now passed in mutual acceptance and friendship in today's generations, with practitioners of both branches exchanging teachings with one-another.

From the USA, Grandmaster Gin-Foon-Mark, student of Lam-Sang, told me personally of Lee-Ying-Sing, and confirmed that he had in fact

With My Si-Fu Grandmaster Lee-Sun-Wah
(Ah-Lien-Gore) Head of the Lee-Yin-Sing Family
and Praying Mantis Kung-Fu Pai

gone back to the Kwangsi Temple and there learned a 'different' version of the Mantis art. Today I enjoy friendly personal relations with Lam –Sang's inheritors under the branches represented in the USA by Grandmaster Mark-Foon (Gin-Foon-Mark) and Grandmaster Henry Poo-Yee.

Also in 1988 I had time to renew my association with Hung-Gar Kung-Fu. This was with Master Chung-Chi-Hung (Mike

Chung). Again, he is very skilled and knowledgeable in Hung-Gar, which was to be recognised in Mainland China by his becoming Technical Director of the Wong-Fei-Hung Kung-Fu Institute – named after Hung-Gar's greatest and most famous practitioner: Wong-Fei Hung.

In July 1988, I had appeared on the front cover of 'Fighters' the martial arts magazine. Things were definitely looking up martial arts wise: but as always happens with any degree of success – jealousies arose and a certain group of non-Chinese people from within the Mantis community tried to blacken my name and my reputation. None of these people however had the guts to face me personally, not even showing up to an arranged face-to-face meeting to 'sort it out'. The Chinese Mantis Masters however, showed their support and acceptance of me: and my would be critics melted away, back once more into obscurity.

I seemed to have gotten over the blow of losing my Police career, and the feeling that had brought of losing a measure of my manhood. This was definitely helped by my martial arts Masters, and at last I began to calm down and draw myself away from non-productive 'challenges' and petty fighting.

Anyway, my application to start Occupational Therapy training had been accepted…

The Occupational Therapy (O.T.) School was located in Liverpool Institute of Higher Education, in Childwall. The course was set at 'professional diploma level' and ran over three years full time. Of the 72 students on that course only six were men, giving a female to male ratio of 11:1. Many men would regard this as heaven: 11 girls to every bloke! Some, definitely took advantage of the 'social choices' available to them. For me however, there was yet another problem: one of adaptation.

In the Police, the situation had been very different. It was a very 'macho' environment – dominated by men and the male psyche.

Here, it was just the opposite. For someone like me who had come suddenly from an atmosphere of screaming testosterone – the blanket oestrogenising effects of a dominant female psyche was a huge culture shock. The polytechnic had been more equally balanced numbers wise, and the martial arts were of course 'masculine' in the broader meaning. Here though, the prevailing spirit was a cross between a Swiss finishing school and a sometimes barely repressed misanthropic feminism.

Still, the academic side was very broad, even if some of the more 'practical' aspects seemed a little gratuitously diversional and perhaps even beside the point.

My Police past followed me to that college. Bullies it seems are everywhere. Get a group of even 6 men together and one of them will try to dominate the rest and become the 'Alpha Male' – number one in the 'baboon troupes' pecking order. Given that there were hordes of available females around to impress, those basic instincts of dominance and aggression must have had much to feed off hormonally. My own 'dominance' activities had been confined to other martial artists – people who were 'up for it' themselves. Here though was a fellow who was a little more primitive – he targeted anyone and everyone.
He was a big bloke, around 6ft 3 tall and heavily built. He had cropped hair, dressed 'hard' and swaggered around. He proudly wore a Marxist red-star badge and boasted of his Masters degree in psychology.

I had nothing to do with him, but all of the other lads either avoided him out of fear, or again out of fear; fell in behind him – thereby getting themselves some 'referred status'. Two of the lads in particular felt intimidated, so, I suggested that they learn some martial arts in order to increase their confidence and personal security. They learned some basic things from me – including how to generate stop-hitting power at close range.

Then, our Bully learned that I'd been in the Police, and even worse that I'd been in the Toxteth riots. He'd been in them too he claimed – on the other 'side'…

'Once a Pig always a Pig!' He declared about me, to his acolytes and the admiring teenage female students. Then followed a whole tirade of abuse about me personally and about the Police in general. My 'friends' told me, and I decided to take action – at an appropriate moment. They though, spilled the beans and warned him that I was a martial arts man – saying that I'd *'Fucking kill him'* – they'd seen what I could do –and he'd better not mess with me. So, he was already primed and I'd lost the initiative. I didn't know how he would react though – and decided to take it as far as I had to. I waited until he was at the head of the que in the canteen. Around him were some of his acolytes and some of the girls. He had his own table – only him and the girls – sitting in splendour like a medieval King. As he paid for his food I stepped up and whispered in his ear:

'You and I are going to have to have a little talk…'

'Wha! What about?'

'About your attitude'

'Wha! Fuck off, don't know what yer mean!'

'About your attitude towards me'.

'I ain't got an attitude!'.

At that point he tried to walk off. I stopped him on his shoulder and whispered into his ear:

'By the way… I'm not a pig'.

At that he whitened and headed off to 'his' table.

Silently, I followed him and sat down – no food just me – opposite him and stared him out as he tried to eat his meal. He lasted less than 10 seconds and then got up and left leaving his own meal unfinished. At that point he'd lost it… beaten psychologically.

I then started getting attention from the girls… which just shows how primitive and ape like all of these behaviours are… he'd lost his status as 'Alpha male' and now apparently I was the 'male interest' on the course! Not my scene any more – maybe years back at Birkenhead Tech!

The best part of the course was the chance to work in hospital environments. We were allocated hospital placements normally, but in the first year you were allowed one 'elective' placement. When Pauline's father Joe, had his first heart attack in 1985, Pauline had written to a very controversial but intriguingly successful cardiac consultant: Dr Peter Nixon, at Charing Cross Hospital in London. Pauline received a very kind reply indicating that Dr Nixon was interested in her Fathers condition and would help. Joe however, declined to take the offer up.

Peter Nixon, was Senior Consultant Cardiologist at the hospital and medical school. He had made a name for himself over the years as being at the cutting edge of new technology – being one of the pioneers in the 1950's of using heart by-pass machines in cardiac surgery. In recent years however, he had developed a whole new regimen of cardiac rehabilitation, which confounded the approaches of regular cardiologists by producing terrific results in people who should have worsened and died. Part of Dr Nixon's approach was to integrate modern science with holistic and complementary therapies – in a 'systems' based way. This was truly scientific medical holism and potentially revolutionary. Dr Nixon's credentials were impeccable, and his enemies in the establishment had a hard time trying to replicate his successes with their supposedly 'orthodox' approaches. Like all pioneers, he made enemies who made things as awkward as possible for him. Dr Nixon however, was a charismatic man, who drew tremendous loyalty and dedication from his hand-picked staff. Together as a team, they worked literal miracles.

Dr Peter Nixon MD FRCP

The O.T.'s in his department were different too, not the somehow second-rate physiotherapists that they sometimes appeared to be in the rest of the National Health Service. Indeed, they were utilised properly by Dr Nixon; and under his guidance, showed their full and true potential as a healing profession. His scientific medicine was augmented by such varied methods as: hypnosis; massage; osteopathy and dance and movement therapies. He had also pioneered the use in cardiology of respiratory psychophysiology, which is the scientific measurement of blood gases in the expired breath of patients as a means to assess their psychological and physiological state. He was a prolific writer and publisher of research in the medical literature…all round, my kind of doctor! I wrote to him and asked if I could undergo a placement at his department. His reply was welcoming, so in July 1988 off I went to Charing Cross hospital cardiac department. It was fated to change the direction of my life and to become a pillar of my future life's work…

Dr Nixon's department was like *nothing* that I had ever seen in any hospital, before or indeed since. Patients were treated like people, in fact that was his staff's watchword: *'turning patients back into people'*. Everyone worked efficiently and effectively towards the real goal of care and rehabilitation. His ward rounds and case conferences were humane – humanistic medicine at its finest. He believed in education for staff and patients with a vast resource of information being made available for all.

He encouraged me to take whatever information I needed and helped me make contact with professors and scientist's world-wide in order to study the new and emerging discipline of general systems theory based, scientific holistic-medicine. I was able to work with the complementary therapists and even to teach some Chi-Gung breathing exercises, and apply John Cain's healing energy to heart patients.

I was particularly interested in his use of hypnosis and the study of trance states with the sick. The effects were so dramatic that I wondered why on Earth are Nixon's method's not used in psychiatry and psychotherapy? Here was an ideal approach to the study of mind-body-environment interrelationships, scientifically, and then applied as a clinical therapy. Dr Nixon became my true therapy mentor – ranked equally in my estimation with my Chinese Kung-Fu Masters. On return to the O.T. College I was a changed man, and what's more there was now no going back….

The O.T. profession had for some decades been trying to find a model of practice that would enable itself to clearly define its role, and to develop in its intuitive direction. Historically, they had been encumbered with the term 'occupation' and had never challenged it. Every argument or debate revolved around that limiting category: What is occupation? What is the meaning of occupation in everyday life? etc. This had meant that they produced theories and models based on a 'special language' understanding of the word: occupation; that had little to do with what the rest of the world thought. Both confusing and themselves confused, the O.T. profession endlessly ruminated about why no one understood them. It didn't seem to have clicked that this was primarily because they didn't understand themselves well enough, to be able to assert their worth and value collectively, as a profession. Hence they always fell into

the shadow of the physiotherapists – whom no one seemed to have a problem understanding – least of all themselves.
The Principal of the O.T. department: Rosemary Barnitt and a senior member of her staff Judith Martin, did seem to grasp the message I brought back from Charing Cross. Both were very supportive of Nixon's ideas and my suggestion that some academic rigour could be applied to it, giving the O.T. profession a new outlook and raison detre. This was great at first, but two things arose that scuppered it all – at least as far as the O.T. profession were concerned.

Firstly, some of the staff at the college seemed keen to appropriate my now developing theoretical work and claim it for themselves. In fact at the World Federation of Occupational Therapist's conference in Australia in 1990, just such a thing was published, 'dumbing down' my role in integrating Dr Nixon's work with professor George Engels' general systems theory based medical model. Professor Engel knew of my development of his ideas and had given it his approval. It seemed that 'students' were not going to be allowed to get beyond themselves. Dr Nixon even wrote and warned me that this would happen. He had attended at the Liverpool O.T. college to give a lecture and had spoken there with some of the staff.

Secondly, Pauline was by now working as a Senior Grade 1 Occupational Therapist in a psychiatric unit. She had introduced the combined Nixon-Engel model, with an additional element of Jungian based psychology that we thought fitted ideally into the framework of the other two as a modern 'psychotherapy'. Pauline had tremendous success with the new approach – pressure testing it against the prevailing methods used in the unit. She stood her ground against the psychiatrists who tried to suggest that it wasn't a 'real' or 'genuine' approach, by citing support from Dr Nixon, Professor Engel, and now from Jungian psychoanalysts' such as Dr Anthony Steven's. It was theoretically sound and in practical terms was proving superior.

The psychiatrists relented and the new 'Systems Therapy' was endorsed by the hospital (Clatterbridege – on the Wirral). However, jealousy from one of Pauline's supervisors, who was 'friends' with a senior member of staff at the O.T. college, meant that a two pronged assault was launched against us. I had passed my second year O.T. exams – no problem, much to the chagrin of some staff members who couldn't understand how I could have done so – when so much of my time was going into developing the new model. Because I am largely self-educated and have been since early childhood, many people make the mistake of thinking that if I haven't learned something from *them* then I *can't* know it! That might be orthodox, but it does not apply with me. It's reminiscent of the Vajranya (Tibetan) tradition in Buddhism, wherein learning can only be 'transmitted' directly from master to pupil. However, being a 'Renaissance' type of fellow, I preferred the Greek tradition, typified by Plato. Here, all knowledge is 'remembering' (anamnesis), and the teachers role is to allow the pupil to discover the truth from within themselves – dialectically. Anyway, I would go anywhere and everywhere that I needed to, to get the requisite knowledge and experience. It's the same in my martial arts also – and I've suffered a similar disservice from some quarters there too.

Miffed, they 'moderated' my exam marks downwards by more than 20% overall, enough to make me fail by 1%. The pass mark being 50%, I was then told that I was spending too much time on Systems Therapy and not enough on the O.T course. Bullshit obviously! Meanwhile, on the same day, Pauline was told that she couldn't practice Systems Therapy anymore in the O.T. department – she'd have to *'tow the line'* with the rest of them. Creativity it seemed was to be stamped out, particularly if it had the temerity to be successful, and to arise from a young husband and wife team.

Well, Pauline and I had been training privately on psychotherapy and hypnosis courses since my placement at

Charing Cross. So, with Dr Nixon's full backing, I decided to leave O.T. and work as a consultant psychotherapist in the NHS, in primary care (front-line as ever) settings. It was at this point that the therapy system was re-named 'Psycho-Systems Analysis Holistic-Medical Psychotherapy'. Accordingly, I told the O.T's to 'stuff it where the Sun don't shine' and resigned from their course, going off to work for G.P's – funded by the local health authority. A few months later Pauline followed suit…

Meanwhile much had been happening elsewhere. Joe, Pauline's Father, had suffered a final and fatal heart attack in December 1988. This upset the equilibrium of her family, and her Mother suddenly came over all dependent, and wanted to *'forget the past'*. However, she began to bleed Pauline emotionally and fell back on trying to re-instate her as her *'baby'*. It took some considerable time to shake off those maledictive influences.
In early, 1989, Master Chan succumbed suddenly to cancer and died. This was an enormous blow to Kung-Fu in Liverpool. Master Chan was a great benefactor to charities and to society in general. He was a truly good man and worthy of respect. He was survived by a widow and two children. During his illness, I had visited with Master Chan at his home, and also in hospital at Clatterbridge on the Wirral. Master Samuel Kwok accompanied me on one such visit, during which Master Chan touchingly acknowledged me as the *'biggest Si-Hing'* under him – meaning in effect his original senior student. He asked Master Kwok to *'look after'* my further Kung-Fu development – formally handing me over to him as his student. Master Kwok has kept faith with his promise to do that, and in return, I still acknowledge Master Kwok as my Si-Fu. Such bonds last longer even than life.

I had known that master Chan was ill, but hadn't seen him for some weeks. Then, one night I had one of those 'John Cain' style dreams, wherein I saw Master Chan glowing with health – at the peak of his physical powers. He was happy and contented

– looking radiant. Sure enough, the following day I telephoned Philip Liu to hear that he had in fact died. A similar thing happened with Joe: there he was as a picture of health, literally glowing. In that dream he asked me to *'look after Pauline and Claire'*. In the dream I promised to… but in outer reality only Pauline could matter and even if I had thought otherwise, Claire's future wasn't in my gift.

I was being exposed to much in the way of oriental spiritualism: 'Sun-Gung' meaning spirit-work as in its development, and'Sun-Dar' meaning spirit attack. For example, in London's China Town, I was approached by a blood Chinese master who was in the Wong-Yuk-Gong lineage of the Mantis system of Kung-Fu, and antithetical to me as he knew that I was in direct line from Grandmaster Lee-Yin-Sing. He immediately stated that he was accompanied by 'Spirits' who would 'kill' me if I tried to harm him! This is pure occultism, maledictive and related to similar things found in the West and in the Caribbean. Much of this comes 'with the turf' of traditional Chinese martial arts – along with acupuncture, traditional medicines, pressure point fighting and so on. This man also dispensed 'yellow paper' curses and hid himself behind a façade of Buddhism, which being a religion of peace and non-violence would itself have nothing to do with such things. Just as in Christianity however, cults of various kinds infect respectable faiths in order to draw vulnerable people (usually Westerners) in. My interest was mainly anthropological – as in how do these practices compare and contrast with those found in the West? Are they real? What is the role of suggestion, psychology and trance states?

Such questions and such experiences have formed a continuous thread in my life since childhood – so I didn't feel as many do that there were 'occult' powers at work – at least not as such. More, it was part of the overall human condition and experience. I was still searching for a unified understanding. One based on any one culture simply wouldn't do for me – it would only be a partial explanation. This viewpoint has always led to misunderstandings towards me, as people who believe in the occult tend to become quite aggressively partisan about their particular system, and alleged insights into a 'higher' truth.

I had realised long-ago that I needed a vantage point from which to weigh up and assess all of these different phenomena and experiences. My base line was Greek rational philosophy – it required proof and evidence beyond superstition. It was not a ‘closed’ or dogmatic system however: it had rigour but at the same time an intuition that soared beyond the obvious. Greek culture was at the foundation of Western philosophy, science and technology.

The classical Greeks were the first peoples anywhere and at any time in history to speak of a cosmopolitan (literally universal civilisation) common to all on the basis of a shared humanity. Their other contributions were quite staggering, many of them subsequently forgotten until rediscovered during the Italian Renaissance and the European scientific revolution.

I realised that as a westerner, any understanding of the East had to come from my own soil – the West, but from that matrix a synthesis was possible, based upon our common and shared humanity. This then was my starting point in drawing together all of my experiences – openness to all phenomena, but, a critical and reflexive methodology applied to their understanding. Greek philosophy was of course the product of a single quite extraordinary culture. However, it had stood the test of time, and scored over other so-called philosophies in being self-critical and self-correcting. That objectivity was the key – it would check itself and indeed demand that such checks be built in. Truth was provisional and subject to review. None of that was characteristic of dogma or bigotry.

I had always been interested in psychology of course – particularly since my early teens, in the work of Carl Gustav

Jung. Jung was classically educated in both sciences and the humanities a true neo-renaissance 'polymath' – someone well educated across the board in many disciplines. His work had the features that I admired and respected: it was based on detailed cross-cultural observations, an understanding of history, of comparative religion, mythology and also of science. His model seemed to explain not only my own somewhat peculiar personality, but also to give a deeper and more meaningful understanding to just about every human situation. Unlike other psychological theories – Jung's method 'travelled', it was applicable in all cultures and places around the world. Jung himself travelled to India, to Africa, and lived and studied with the indigenous North American Indians' long before the collective cultural conscience in The USA made it a fashionable thing to do. He wrote the first Western forewords to Suzuki's series of essays on Zen Buddhism. He wrote a foreword to the first English language translation of the Chinese 'Book of Changes' the 'I-Ching'. His knowledge was truly vast and acquired over 65 years of professional practice. I had applied Jung's ideas to myself – in a pressure testing way since my teens. Jung himself had undergone an extensive 'self-analysis' facing the full fury of the human psyche's ability to produce mental illness, superstition, the occult and so-forth. He was an ideal 'mentor' for my personal project of self-development.

In psychotherapy practice, Pauline and I applied Jung's ideas and techniques clinically as part of the overall systems theory based approach of Dr Nixon and professor Engel. We worked at several G.P.'s practices: and getting to-date (at the time of writing) experience of working with over 1,000 people in depth on some of the most horrendously difficult and convoluted personal, social and medical problems. Many of these were 'mind-body interactive', showing how the state of one affects that of the other. Many were 'Religious' problems – in the broader sense of needing to find meaning in life and a way of making sense of things.

A significant number have suffered from the effects of superstition, magical thinking, the occult and maledictive suggestion. As a result, I have been 'spiritually attacked' by Witches of all kinds; 'Black Magic' practitioners – Eastern as well as Western –all in the service of maintaining their destructive hold over vulnerable people. Fortunately, my training and life experience have prepared me to face such assaults, as they were in everyday understanding quite frankly 'evil' intending to cause me and my family harm or even death. We have been able to help in drawing people back from the brink of self-destruction, and worked closely and in co-operation with doctors to assist in the alleviation, and in some cases apparent 'cure', of diseases and of disease processes. Pauline and I have published research on psychotherapy, occupational therapy and respiratory psychophysiology. This last one resulted in me being nominated for entry to *Who's Who in America*: World, Science and Medicine editions.

We have been at the heart of the psychotherapy and also complementary medicine fields, acting as National Occupational Standards consultants for psychotherapy and clinical hypnosis. I now hold a number of consultative positions on professional therapy bodies, including the Institute for Complementary Medicine (ICM) in London.

In 1998, I published two professional papers; following their presentation at an international conference on martial arts research at the Sports and Exercise Science faculty of Manchester Metropolitan University. These were: *'Hyperventilation, trance states and suggestion in the martial arts';* and, *'From post modernism to dialectical syncretism: understanding the anthropology and cultural evolution of martial arts systems'*. That same year I became a Founder Fellow of the Society of Martial Arts (FSMA) as inaugurated by Dr Eugene de Silva and Professor David Collins.

2000 saw the publication of my first book: 'Hop-Gar Mantis Kung-Fu a science of combat'. This was an essential bridge for me to organise my ideas and experiences in the combined fields of psychology, philosophy and the martial arts. It was received with great critical acclaim and acted as a manifesto for my now inevitable development of a 'Pan East-West global martial art'. Long before, in the late 1960's, as a student of Japanese Wado-Ryu Karate, I had been intrigued to read in a

Receiving my Founder Fellowship award (FSMA) of the Society of Martial Arts from Tom Hibbert MBE at the Manchester Metropolitan University Sports & Exercise Science Faculty: July 1998

book by the great Karate Master Tatsuo Suzuki (Karate-Do. pub. Pelham Books 1967) of a Western martial tradition that went all the way back to the ancient Greeks, and was indeed an Olympic combat sport in the 7th century BC! This combat art was 'Pankration' the name being made up from the Greek words: pan meaning 'all' and kratos: meaning 'power', 'strength' or 'force'. Therefore, Pankration was a martial combat art that included the use of any and all forms of technique and power. The later developments of western boxing and wrestling were taken from the Pankration and distilled into sports. The historical origins of Pankration disappear back into the mists of time, back to the 'Heroic' age of Greece and the times of Homer's Trojan War period (around 1300 BC). In legend, its founder was the hero and demi-god Heracles (Hercules) or sometimes; Theseus: the famous hero who slew the half-man half-bull monster in the Labyrinth at the palace of Knossos on the island of Crete.

Pankration was more than just an Olympic event however, it formed the basis for all combat training for Greek soldiers – including the famous Spartan Hoplite warriors and Alexander the Greats' Macedonian Phalanx troops. The techniques of Pankration varied just as in the oriental martial arts, according to 'style'. These specific Pankration systems were taught within families or directly from master-teachers (Thaskalos) to their fighting students (Pankratists). Many features common in oriental arts were to be found: forms or 'Kata' known as 'Pyrrics; single-blow challenges called the 'Klimax'; the use of punch bags and wooden posts for striking and the hardening of the body and limbs through beatings and the application of herbal medicines; internal energy development through breathing exercises 'pneuma' (the equivalent of Chi and Chi-Gung in the traditional Chinese arts).

Pankration spread eastwards across the world with Greek culture in general, through the conquests of Alexander the Great, reaching as far as India, Afghanistan and even to the gates of the Chinese Empire itself. Many martial arts historians, notably Suzuki (above) but also Kanazawa and Oyama, openly suggest that the Pankration actually influenced the development of Indian, Chinese and eventually Okinawan and Japanese martial arts. This is of course very controversial, as much national and cultural pride is held to be at stake. What is absolutely certain is that Greek culture which dominated much of India for the next four centuries also affected the culture of the Asian Steppes and at least in terms of perspective art – China itself. The Greeks of this period, known as the 'Hellenistic Age' absorbed just about as much as they introduced to those oriental cultures – laying the foundation for realising the philosopher Aristotle's dream of a world civilisation based on Greek culture. Naturally, this process would have extended to the Pankration, and we should expect therefore that the oriental arts encountered in battle by

Alexander's army would have been absorbed into the Pankration as much as the Pankration was to affect the development of Kalari (literally: 'Battleground') – the indigenous martial art of the Indian Sub-Continent.

By the Roman period in Europe, the Pankration was known by its Latin name: Pancratium – and became the basis for gladiatorial training at such places as Capua, Pompeii and the Colosseum itself. Thus the Pankration continued on into the Christian era, only disappearing when the last gladiator schools and the Ancient Olympic games themselves where abolished and closed down by the Christians in the 5th century AD (along with all the classical Greek universities, libraries and museums). Thus paradoxically, the 'Dark Ages' – the extinction of classical culture and learning in the former Western Roma Empire was ushered in by the Christians, and not by the much maligned Teutonic barbarians: the Goths and Vandals, nor indeed by that scourge from the Asian Steppe; Attila The Hun… Ironically, it was to be Muslim culture that preserved much of the lost Greek heritage eventually returning it to the West during the Italian Renaissance.

During the middle ages, elements of the Pankration survived in Europe as much watered down arts such as Greco-Roman wrestling, boxing, as well as in the more practical and combative systems of La-Savate (French kick-boxing) and similar methods still found today in Spain and Portugal. Pankration has seen a revival since the 1960's with various systems arising as once again Westerners become aware of their formidable martial arts heritage. This was perhaps inevitable, with the influx of oriental arts that has occurred since World war II. Many modern Pankration systems have been developed as versions of the currently popular 'No holds barred' or 'Ultimate Fighting Challenge' (UFC) competitions. As an often 'fight-to-the-death' event, Pankration was the original and perhaps most formidable of all 'Mortal Combat' systems.

Some systems of modern Pankration however, are orientated towards street self-defence and personal self-development – easily rivalling the Eastern martial arts in technical ability and spiritual/philosophical insight. I created a new Pankration school: the 'Renaissance Pankration Academy', so named after the re-discovery of Classical (Greek) learning that marked the end of the High Medieval period or 'Middle ages' in Europe: the Italian Renaissance. It takes its inspiration from a *contemporary* rediscovery of the classical European martial arts and philosophical heritage, particularly that of Alexander the Great and the martial spirit of the Ancient Olympic games.
Just as Alexander freely incorporated Asian culture into his primarily Greek learning, so the Renaissance Pankration school freely adopts and incorporates oriental martial techniques and styles into its fundamentally European, Classical Greek philosophy and combat system.

Thus I have come full circle, having started in the West with Boxing and Western Science; then going East into Karate and classical Chinese martial arts, and finally, returning once more enriched immeasurably by the journey; to European Pankration and Classical Greek philosophy.

The Academy jointly headed by myself and that fine martial artist Brian McKinney, is a recognised branch of the 'Union Internationale de Pancrasse': the International Union of Pankration and Allied Disciplines (IUPAD), and the European Federation of Pankration (EFP). These bodies exist to promote and regulate the art of Pankration and have a world-wide membership. The Academy is also a member of the British Combat Association (BCA), one of the World's premier organisations dedicated to practical combat martial arts and self-protection training. The BCA was founded by my friends: Peter Consterdine and Geoff Thompson, two of the very finest Western martial artists and world class experts in the field of practical combat. The Academy has spread overseas now with two established branches in the USA headed by John F.

Springer of Maryland. John is a very accomplished martial artist - both 'traditionally' within Chinese Kung-Fu, and more broadly in military terms as a former US Special Forces soldier. John's background which includes an excellent education in Western classical (Greek) culture and philosophy together with his impeccable martial arts and real world experience make him the ideal head of the USA Pankration Academy. In Australia, 'Aussie' John Lee heads the Renaissance Pankration Academy, teaching a variety of traditional and more modern martial arts. Beyond martial arts techniques, the Academies students have the opportunity to study Hellenic (Classical Greek) culture and philosophy. External academic validation of educational courses in philosophy are being produced, to encourage students to develop the moral and ethical side of their studies in a way that embodies the spirit of Socrates, Plato and Aristotle, and that of the Renaissance Florentine Academy in Italy.

Three significant events have really impacted me over recent years: Firstly, the birth to Pauline of my children: a Son Gareth and a Daughter Rhiannon. They are an incredible blessing and loved deeply and sincerely.

Secondly, my martial arts career has culminated in my being accepted by Praying Mantis Kung Fu Grandmaster Lee-Lien as his disciple and a nominated co-successor (with Andy Liu-Kin-Ming, son of Philip Liu and Nephew of my first Kung-Fu teacher: Kenneth Liu-Ying-Wah) – an unprecedented accolade for a non-Chinese to succeed in direct line from a Chinese Grandmaster. This irks many of my critics who still don't understand how I can unite the twin threads of East and West into a single whole, without compromise to either –based on our deeper and shared common human heritage.

Lastly, for Pauline and I: the invitation from Franz Jung the son of Carl Jung, to visit with him at his late Fathers' home in Zurich Switzerland, during 1992. Franz was the literal 'keeper' of his Father's heritage. We had written to him, as apparently many hundreds had, in the hope of making a visit and of paying our respects to his Father's memory. We explained how much his Father had influenced our lives, and how we had integrated his work with scientific-holistic medicine in order to bring Jungian therapy to those ordinary folk who in their suffering of the soul had most deserved it and yet were the least likely to receive it.

Franz replied that he received many letters, but an 'intuition' from the unconscious told him to reply and to invite us to his home. The house itself was beautiful, designed by Carl Jung himself. Inside were his library and study where he worked with his patients from 1907 to 1961.

It was an incredible privilege to be welcomed into a home that had seen such visitors as Albert Einstein and Sigmund Freud. Franz was a dignified figure: with a still, and penetrative gaze – looking the mirror image of his Father. He listened carefully to what we had achieved, but before saying anything else in reply he asked a core Jungian question:

'Tell me of your childhood dreams'.

I did...

Franz listened and something about the whole situation turned as if through a deep understanding. What followed is beyond my ability to put into writing, but the result was a blessing for our project and a personal friendship with Franz himself that lasted until his death.

Jungians will understand the significance of that visit. It was all as it was *intended* to be by the psyche – even from the very beginning...long ago...

Gareth & Rhiannon

With Pauline & Herr Franz Jung: at home in his Fathers study: Kustnact Lake Zurich Switzerland; May 2nd 1992

Reflections

"An unexamined life is not worth living" Socrates.

The best thing about middle-age, it seems to me, is that you have by now lived enough of a life to possess a sense of meaning and of continuity. In my work as a psychotherapist, I often find that people who have lost their way in life have lost contact with the thread of their essential spirit, their *personal myth:* those things that cannot be given up without losing hold of what it means to be yourself. This 'thread', leads in most cases back to childhood, and around it gather the most significant events of our lives. It is an unfolding narrative that reaches its conclusion in its own conscious understanding by we ourselves. Looking back, everything that has happened thus far in my life was prefigured in my early childhood. My interest in the human psyche: literally in Greek, the *'soul'* was predominant even then. The need to be both a part of nature *and* to attempt an understanding of it objectively where mirrored in my relationship to my Mother and Father respectively. The tension created by the divisions between these opposites called for a search for unity: of mind and body, of East and West.

My career in the police was absolutely necessary for my development. It balanced what would otherwise have been a too spiritual or even an aesthetic approach to life. Police work tests as perhaps no other arena of human life can: in it there is no escaping the mundane but irreducible physical realities of life and of death. It forces us to dig deep into our very being – facing our limitations as well as our potentials for heroism, for cowardice, for self-sacrifice and self-preservation. Whereas war is of course the ultimate 'collective' experience, Policing tests the 'individual' as you are just as often rejected as accepted by the society that you serve. That inevitable and daily alienation from the rest of humanity is part of the heroism of ordinary Police Officers. I retain the greatest respect for those men and women; people who would unflinchingly lay down their lives for a stranger. Each struggle, each wrong turning along my journey, cut and shaped my roughly hewn personality into its final yet prefigured form. I *had* to take the path that I did, I had no choice in it at all. The Greeks understood this process as 'teleology' which essentially means that the goal is present at the beginning and draws us towards it, kicking and screaming maybe – but inexorably – most assuredly.

Jung said: *'The future casts its shadow backwards and takes shape in the present'*. How true… Socrates, that greatest of all Greek philosophers, and role model for the inquirer into knowledge said: *'An unexamined life is not worth living'*.
In examining myself back over these last forty five years, I find that I have an Anglo-Celt soul, but with a soaring Greek spirit that has built a physical and psychological bridge between that ultimate pair of cultural opposites: oriental East and occidental West. That it seems has been my task — and perhaps, one for others also…

Adverts

Will the reader please note that the following advertising section of the book is included to let you know of other Self Protection related merchandise.
You the reader, have not been charged for the printing or paper used in this section. The cost for this has been absorbed by New Breed Publishing.
The price that you have paid for this publication is for the knowledge, information and advice given by Steve Richards throughout the rest of this book.
Thank you

IN YOUR FACE - 'CLOSE QUARTER FIGHTING'
By Kevin O'Hagan
£14 from **NEW BREED**
WWW.NEWBREEDBOOKS.CO.UK

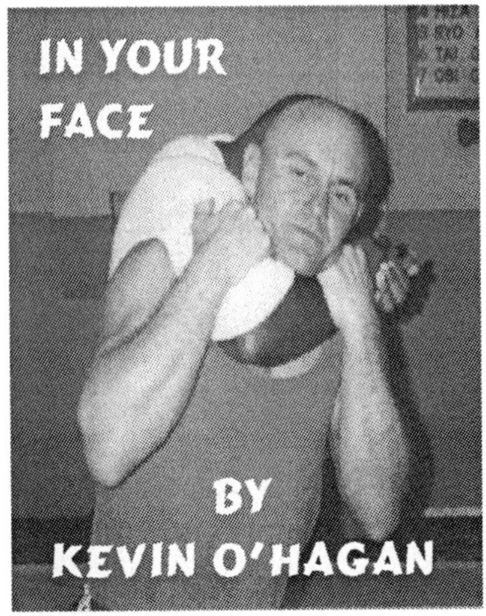

Coming soon
Future NEW BREED publications
By Steve Richards

THUGS
MUGS
AND
VIOLENCE
Want to know what its like
when it really kicks off?
Forget the movies - this is the REAL world.
Jamie O'Keefe
www.newbreedbooks.co.uk

GRAPPLING
WITH
REALITY
SURVIVAL ON THE GROUND
KEVIN O'HAGAN